In His Shoes

In His Shoes

A Short Journey Through Autism

Joanna L. Keating-Velasco

APC
P.O. Box 23173
Shawnee Mission, Kansas 66283-0173
www.asperger.net

© 2008 Autism Asperger Publishing Co.
P. O. Box 23173
Shawnee Mission, Kansas 66283-0173
www.asperger.net

Publisher's Cataloging-in-Publication

Keating-Velasco, Joanna L.
    In his shoes : a short journey through autism / Joanna L. Keating-Velasco. -- 1st ed. -- Shawnee Mission, Kan. : Autism Asperger Pub. Co., c2008.

        p. ; cm.
        ISBN: 978-1-934575-26-0
        LCCN: 2008928393
        Audience: Middle-school.
        Summary: Through a fictionalized story of a year in the life of 13-year-old Nick Hansen, young readers are exposed to some of the challenges faced by a teenager with autism. The emphasis is on how we are more similar than different and ways to accommodate the views of individuals with autism. Each chapter includes a discussion guide.

        1. Autism in adolescence--Juvenile literature. 2. Autistic youth--Juvenile literature. 3. Social interaction in youth--Juvenile literature. 4. [Autism.] I. Title.

RJ506.A9 K435 2008   2008928393
618.92/85882--dc22   0806

Cover Art: © iStockPhoto; ernestking

Illustrations ©2007 JupiterImages Corporation

This book is designed in American Typewriter and Times New Roman.

Printed in the United States of America.

You're a child of few words,

With a heart made of gold.

You've got something to say,

Let your story be told.

– Joanna L. Keating-Velasco

Not being able to speak is not the same thing as having nothing to say.

– Author Unknown

Acknowledgments

Jeff & Kristina Velasco
For continued support in my pursuit
of promoting autism awareness.

Mom & Dad
For always fully supporting everything I do.

Kirsten McBride – My Editor
For always taking what I have written and
helping me transform it into what I only
dreamed it could be.

Debbie Hall
For sharing her strength and experience
and offering a mother's perspective on autism.

Corinne Escobar-Griffiths
For taking me under her wings and being
an enthusiastic mentor.

Zosia Zaks
For giving me the encouragement I needed
at just the right time.

Linda & Nancy
Two incredible moms with amazing hearts.

Webmaster G, Pat Grimm
Yikes, I'd be technologically lost without you!

My Colleagues at PYLUSD
For the lessons and laughter you provide
every day.

The Rainbow of Students
who have been true inspirations and heroes to me.

Once again, dedicated to
my friend, Jon.

Finally, thank you, God,
for opening so many doors of opportunity
for me to promote autism awareness!

Preface

The privilege of spending the past eight years working in classrooms with students who have autism has opened my heart to their unique qualities and gifts. As an instructional aide, I am able to spend quality one-on-one time with students and learn about their individual challenges, talents and personalities. They teach me so many more life lessons daily than I could ever imagine teaching them.

Autism is a neurological (brain) disorder that ranges in severity and is defined by challenges in three major areas: language, social interaction and restricted patterns of behavior. Autism is a spectrum disorder, meaning the symptoms and characteristics may present themselves in a wide variety of combinations, from mild to severe. The spectrum ranges from those who are severely challenged, less able and dependent on others, to those who have above-average intelligence and are independent, yet may experience sensory issues and find society's view of social skills tricky.

According to the Centers for Disease Control and Prevention (CDC) in 2007, an average of 1 in 150 children are diagnosed on the autism spectrum, and autism is four times more common in boys than in girls. It is imperative that we strive to understand these children – their wants, hopes and dreams. Also, I feel it is our responsibility to educate their peers and the wider community to encourage mutually beneficial relationships.

In His Shoes is my attempt to provide vignettes of activities and situations kids with autism may face throughout a school year – activities and situations that are mostly the same as those other kids experience, but from a different perspective. How much more we would all learn if we could just spend a moment "walking in the shoes" of a child with autism! Our main character, Nicholas Hansen, is a 13-year-old boy who has autism. At school, he is enrolled in a self-contained class that serves as a hub for integrating in and out of various classes to learn, socialize and interact with "neurotypical" kids in the general student population.

Since I don't experience autism personally, I hope that through my research, discussions with individuals who have autism, my day-to-day experience with students, as well as discussions with families of kids on the spectrum, I can provide a forum for discussion about autism. I don't profess to be an expert, but I do feel called to increase autism awareness to the best of my ability.

My hope is that after reading this, when you interact with individuals who have autism you will ...
- Discover and support their unique talents and gifts
- Support their interests while encouraging areas where interest may be lacking
- Direct obsessive interests or passions into projects that they enjoy
- Respect their many sensory issues and challenges
- Help them cope in society without changing the core of who they are
- Witness the unique gifts, talents and characteristics autism presents from a fresh perspective
and,
- *Especially,* attempt to put yourself "in their shoes" – if even for a moment.

JK-V

Table of Contents

Good Morning, Sunshine

Through the branches of the palm tree outside, sun filtered into the kitchen, casting dancing shadows across the walls. As Nicholas sat at the kitchen table watching the shadows, he thought, *First breakfast, then waterfall. I wish dad could take me.*

Nick's family was away for a few days visiting some colleges that his sister, Karen, was considering attending in the fall. Usually Nick traveled with the family, but this particular trip would be a whirlwind of boring meetings and wouldn't be fun for him at all. He was bummed that his family was away. It's not that he wanted to be there. He just missed them. But he felt lucky that Kris, his favorite sitter, was with him. She was busy cooking, and it smelled awesome.

While she cooked, Kris sang one of Nick's favorite songs, "You are my sunshine, my only sunshine …" Occasionally, if she paused, he would join in with a word or two. Nick liked Kris. She didn't just "sit" on him the way the word "sitter" sent images through his mind. She enjoyed spending time and interacting with him. Every day she asked, "Hey buddy, where should Club Nick venture off to today?"

Nick giggled as he thought, *Club Nick. I like that.* While his mom, and dad and sister were away, he got a little vacation of his own since Kris took him to all of his favorite places – the beach, the park, the train station, the science museum – much more fun than trailing behind Karen to admissions offices on college campuses … oh, and In-N-Out Burger, of course! *Yum, double-double burger, fries and a shake. Mmmm.* Just thinking about it made his mouth water. He breathed in through his nose and smelled bacon.

As for family vacations, Nick had a love/hate relationship with them. He loved to see the new places and spend time with his family, but sometimes he found it difficult to deal with the changes in schedule, the new experiences and all of the unknowns.

A shiny strip of paper on the table caught Nick's eyes. The top of it read, "Club Nick – Tuesday." It showed a picture of the lake labeled "PARK," followed by a picture of a McDonald's marked "LUNCH." Below was a series of other pictures, including a video store, a snack, a swimming pool, dinner, and a computer. The last one was a picture of his bed marked "SLEEP." Club Nick – Tuesday looked promising!

"Clank, bang, ting" went the pots and pans as Kris finished preparing Nick's breakfast.

Staring off, Nick ran some wonderful numbers through his head, *1, 2, 4, 8, 16, 32, 64, 128, 256* ... He enjoyed doubling numbers and seeing them get bigger and bigger and bigger as he pictured them expanding in his mind. He loved numbers. They were so dependable.

Soon Kris headed his way with a plate full of food. Nick's eyes widened with anticipation. A growl echoed in his stomach. Putting the plate down in front of him, Kris announced, "There you go, Nicholas. It's all for you, buddy." Then she sat down to read the newspaper while Nick ate his breakfast.

Nick sat staring at the plate. With a giant breath in, he inhaled the delicious aroma. *Mmmmm.* He saw eggs, toast, bacon and – sliced apples? *Oh, no!* He was so hungry, and the smells during the cooking had seemed so yummy. But there it was – the repulsive image right in front of him. Although there were also some of his favorite foods staring at him, just the sight of the red skin on the apples made him feel nauseous.

He tried to look at the toast instead. Perfect symmetry. The bread was cut into precise triangles and topped with an exact square of butter ready for him to spread. The bacon was cooked crispy, and the eggs were prepared sunny side up, just the way he liked them. He loved the big yellow circles, which reminded him of the warm sunshine. He enjoyed popping them with his fork and mentally sensing the warmth of the sun on his body as they oozed onto his plate.

"No red," he said quietly.

Kris put down the paper and looked up. "What did you say? Sorry, I couldn't hear you."

No response.

Nick kept trying to look at the positive of what was on the plate in front of him. *Hmmm. The foods are not touching ... good. RED apples, yuck!* It's not that he didn't like the taste of apples. Applesauce and apple pie were delicious. But to put such an offensive color on his plate with other foods could not be tolerated. Crinkling his nose, he wondered, *Why would Kris serve me red food? It is infecting my whole plate. Gross.* In a gruff voice, he groaned louder, "No!"

He looked up at Kris. He liked Kris. He knew that she was trying to be nice to him as she reminded him, "Nick, it's time to eat." Her voice was calm and cheerful, which he had learned to associate with the emotion of happiness.

How could she not know that red, sliced apples were visually the most offensive food on the planet? *I wish mom was here. She would say, "Kris, peel off the red skin and cut the apple into small chunks. Problem solved!" Or, How about green apples?*

Well, somehow he was going to have to let Kris in on this "secret of life." Seconds passed as he stared at the awful sight in front of him, trying to figure out how to tell Kris about this problem.

The challenge facing Nick was that he had autism and was practically nonverbal. He rarely spoke, and when he did speak, usually his words were not understood or particularly relevant to those around him. Sometimes he just echoed what other people said.

"No, No, No."

"No, what, Nick?" Kris asked, still trying to figure out the problem.

Nick stared at the apple slices, unpleasant as it made him feel, and with a shifting of his eyes, tried to will them off his plate. It didn't work. He squeezed his eyes tightly shut and saw pictures of apples disappearing from his plate flashing across his mind. Full of hope he opened his eyes, but they were still there.

"NOOOOOOOO!" he screamed this time. Frustrated, he began flapping his arms, hoping Kris would understand his predicament.

But she just stared at him, unable to understand why he was becoming agitated. *Why isn't he eating? I know he's hungry.* Nick kept pushing the plate away, hoping Kris would just remove the apples so he could start enjoying the rest of the breakfast. Gently, she pushed it back saying, "Come on, Nick. I know you're hungry. Hurry up so we can go to the park."

She just doesn't get it. Nick was becoming so frustrated that he felt like he was going to burst. He tried to speak the pictures and words that floated in his head, but couldn't get the words to come out properly. He felt like a volcano ready to erupt, but only odd noises exploded from his lips.

Kris saw him becoming increasingly agitated and frustrated, but *frustrated over what*, she wondered? Frantic to help, she looked around the room for his communication book. "Dang it. Where is that book!?" she whispered nervously to herself. The pictures in the book might help Nick tell her what he wanted and what was wrong. "That book is his voice. Where is it?!" she mumbled.

Seconds passed as Nick tried to think of a way to let Kris know the problem. Meanwhile, his anxiety kept escalating until finally he picked up his plate and hurled it on the floor. "CRASH!" The food splattered everywhere, including Nick's favorite Converse shoes.

In His Shoes

The yellow yolks had exploded and were dripping down from his shoes to the floor. As he watched the yolk trickle down from his shoes, he screamed in frustration. Then he began sobbing. After a few minutes, he was so exhausted he slowly made his way to his bean bag chair tracking egg yolk along the way. He plopped down into the bean bag and let out a heavy sigh.

In the meantime, Kris stood near the table with her mouth open – still totally confused by what just occurred. Not knowing what else to do, she started to clean up the mess, giving Nick a few minutes to relax on the beanbag chair.

"Nick, I know you're hungry. Would you like some Frosted Flakes?" Hearing that, Nick came back to the kitchen table and rapidly shoveled the cereal into his mouth. After Nick finished, Kris put his bowl into the sink. Then she picked up the "Club Nick – Tuesday" schedule from the table and touched the picture of the park.

"Let's go, Nick."

"Park," he replied as he got up from the table. Together, they headed out the front door toward the park.

As they approached the park entrance, Kris said, "Hmmm, I still don't understand what upset you so much about breakfast, buddy? Are you feelin' okay?" She paused, hoping for a reply. Finally, she said, "I wish you could tell me, Nick. I know you've got something to say."

Nick stared down at the ground and let out a barely audible sigh. Dust from the path clung to the remaining egg yolk on his shoes. He still felt irritated that he had trouble communicating his thoughts to Kris. As they walked along the path toward the waterfall, Kris put her hand out toward Nick. He accepted it and squeezed back in reply.

POINTS TO PONDER ...

- How do you think it would feel to be unable to express your feelings and thoughts so that others could understand you? How would you have reacted in this situation if you had been Nick?

- Have you ever been in a situation where you were very frustrated because those around you could not understand what you were going through or how you felt? Perhaps you lost your voice or were in a place where no one spoke your language.

- How did Nick communicate his frustration?

- Have you ever been in contact with someone who was unable to speak or communicate with you effectively? How did that feel? What did you do to help? What ways did you or the other person use to communicate without using words?

Extra! Extra!

A s the end of summer approached, the community center was bubbling over with activity. Teens rode up on skateboards and bikes from every direction, practically flying into the building.

"Beeeeep, beeeeep, beeeeep," warned the van as it backed up to the side entrance of the building to drop off newspapers. Kids sprang through the double doors to unload the stacks of papers for their weekly newspaper routes. The community center was a bustling place for youth during the summer months and continued to remain active in the afternoons once the school year resumed. Over the school holidays, the center offered free or low-cost activities for the local teens and a variety of job opportunities to help them earn a little money.

A young man wearing a name badge that read "Jim Alan" slowly eased by the crowd of kids unloading papers from the van. He paused in front of the center, looked at his watch and waited. Jim was Nick's job coach at the community center this summer. In addition to coordinating the teen activities, he was hired to help support Nick in whatever job or activity the kids were involved each day. At night, he attended the local university where he was studying to be a speech pathologist.

Soon he noticed a car entering the parking lot. The passenger window was open, and he saw Nick's head leaning out. Jim smiled. As the car pulled up, Nick's mom waved while Nick pulled his head back into the car and started to open the door. "Hey Nick, are you ready to get to work?" Jim greeted him.

"Ready to work?" Nick repeated as he unbuckled his seat belt and fully opened the car door.

Jim lifted up his hand for a high-five, and Nick responded by slapping it back. Nick smiled, thinking, *I like Jim. He's nice.* They had worked together all summer and had gained a great deal of respect for each other. Jim did his best to recognize and interpret Nick's needs. He never talked down to him and always spoke to him as if he understood everything he said. He respected Nick's space, physically, and never touched him without warning or permission. He had learned that the sense of touch, at times, made Nick anxious. Best of all, Jim often told funny stories that made Nick laugh. Jim was never totally sure if Nick really thought he was funny or if he just knew somehow when it was an appropriate time to laugh. Either way, Nick was a great audience for Jim's humor.

Carrying his communication book, Nick slipped by Jim and trotted toward the front entrance while Jim waved a quick goodbye to Nick's mom.

"Toot, toot," she honked back and drove off to work.

As they entered the center, Nick looked at the large daily calendar on the bulletin board. It was written in words and illustrated in large pictures.

Monday's job read "RECYCLE" over a picture of bottles and soda cans. Tuesday's activity read "WATER DAY" and pictured squirt guns and a water slide. Wednesday's job read "PAPER ROUTE" and showed a stack of rolled up newspapers. Thursday's activity showed "MOVIE DAY" and displayed a DVD next to movie snacks. Lastly, Friday listed "LIBRARY JOBS" with a picture of books on shelves.

Nick was greeted by other teens as he moved past them toward the calendar board. He did not respond to their greetings. So, Jim gently guided him back in their direction, reminding him to say, "Hi." Turning back to the calendar, Jim pointed to Wednesday and said, "It's paper route day, Nick."

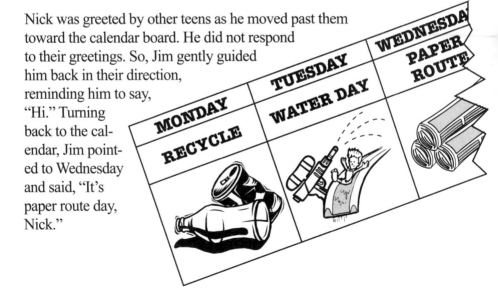

In His Shoes

"Paper route," he repeated. *Yes! My favorite day! I love to roll and deliver the papers.* He put down his communication book and followed Jim out to the van to get papers for their route. Jim helped Nick count out 65 papers. Then Nick carried his stack back into the center and plopped them onto a table.

"Are you still earning money for those new shoes, Nick?" asked Jim as he grabbed a handful of rubber bands. "You 'oughta be getting close. How much do you have in your jar?"

"In your jar?" Nick repeated. Grinning, he looked across the room to the desk, spying "Nick's Money" jar with the picture of a pair of shoes taped onto it. Last time they were here, he had counted the money and remembered, *$30.42 and counting! Almost there.* "Shoes."

Nick had found an advertisement for a pair of shoes in a sports magazine that he and Jim were browsing through earlier in the month. With the money he earned from various community center jobs, he had chosen to work toward purchasing those shoes.

"That's right, Nick. Gotta earn your new shoes. Let's get to work." Jim started rolling papers and inserting them into a special container that held the rolled paper tightly upright so that Nick could place a rubber band around it. Then Nick would take each tightly rolled paper and put it into his delivery bag.

As Nick and Jim continued to roll their papers as a team, most of the other teens had finished their stacks and were leaving to start their various routes.

"Hey, Jim," said Shannon while picking up her full delivery bag.

"What's up?" Jim replied.

Extra! Extra!

"Ian and Eric didn't show up again, but I rolled and bagged their route so it's ready to go," answered Shannon.

Jim sighed and shook his head. "Thanks, Shannon. I appreciate your help. Nick and I will take their job if they don't show up soon. He can use the extra money for his jar."

"Okay, see ya later, Jim. Bye, Nick!" yelled Shannon as she grabbed her helmet and skateboard, heading out the door.

Nick looked up and waved back. *Bye, Shannon.*

As Nick was finishing rubber banding his last few papers, Jim commented, "Wow, they all got out of here fast today! I gotta go re-park the van before we go on our route. I'll be right back." Jim headed out the side entrance toward the van.

Just as Jim had left, two boys on bikes skidded to an abrupt stop at the front entrance of the community center. Before entering, they dropped their bikes, causing Nick to notice and look up at them.

Ian slid in first on his Heelys, yelling back to the other boy, "Yo, Eric, look! It's Not-So-Quick-Nick!"

Soon Eric entered the room. Noticing that no one else was around, he replied, "Oooh, that's slick, Ian!" They both laughed. "Hey, looks like someone rolled our papers for us again. Ha!"

Ian replied, "Awesome!"

Nick ignored them and finished packing his papers into his bag – until they started messing around with his money jar. Quietly, he watched in horror as Eric opened the jar and started running his hands through the change and counting the bills. "Dude, look at all this! We could do some serious damage at the mall with this."

In His Shoes

Getting angry, Nick began mumbling, "Not all treasure is silver and gold, mate," over and over, repeating a scene he recalled from *The Pirates of the Caribbean* movie. The repetition helped calm him while he tried to decide what to do. He attempted to tell the boys to leave his jar alone, but only odd-sounding noises left his mouth.

"Bla, bla, bla, is all I hear when you talk, Nick. You kill me, dude," teased Eric.

Both boys looked at Nick. Suddenly Ian got an idea. "Dude, what do you need this money for anyway? Your mom will buy you whatever you want. Stupid rich kid!" Ian moved towards Nick. Grabbing Nick's chin and facing Nick's eyes directly into his, he demanded, "HEY! Look at me when I'm talking to you, moron!"

Moron. "No," replied Nick jerking his chin back and looking away. Eye contact frightened him. Plus, he had trouble concentrating on listening while making eye contact. The way Ian held his chin startled him, making his body feel like it was being attacked. He was listening to what they were saying about his money and becoming furious. "NO!!"

"No – that's all you have to say. You are a man of few words, dude," commented Ian sarcastically.

"NOOOOOOO!" Nick yelled, repeating the only thing he was able to utter at the moment.

Eric laughed, made a goofy face and mimicked, "Noooo!"

Through the window, Ian saw Jim returning. "Crap! Jim's coming back. Get your bag and let's go!" Then he grabbed his delivery bag, dumped Nick's money jar into it and skidded out the exit. The boys scrambled onto their bikes and rode off, smiling and waving at Jim as they passed him.

Extra! Extra!

Surprised to see them, Jim waved back with a concerned look on his face. *Oh great, what are they up to now?* He looked up at the community center and saw Nick's silhouette in the doorway.

Staring out the door, Nick stood thinking, *what do they need my money for? They already have nice shoes.* A solitary tear crept down his cheek as he watched his hard-earned money disappear into the distance. He felt helpless. Seeing them pass Jim as they left, he wondered, *why didn't Jim stop them?* He wanted to yell out, but the words just wouldn't flow.

Sensing something was wrong, Jim rushed back into the room. "What happened?! Nicholas, what's wrong? What did they do?" Nick bolted to the corner and began furiously biting his hand. "Nicholas, STOP! You are going to hurt yourself." Jim was getting angry at himself for not being there for Nick. He took a deep breath to calm himself. Then he slowly said, "Okay, deep breaths, Nick. It's going to be okay. Relax."

"Relaaaaax!" Nick yelled. *RELAX?! Why should I relax? They just stole my money!* Now completely frustrated with the situation, he continued to scream and bit harder on his hand.

Without another word, Jim pointed Nick toward his favorite chair. But Nick didn't budge, only continued screaming. Jim turned off the radio that had been blaring, trying to create a calmer environment for Nick. Again he pointed to the comfortable chair. Finally, Nick's screaming turned into crying as he headed to the chair and plopped down. He stopped biting his hand and continued crying, but he slowly began to relax. Finally, he took a deep breath and exhaled in exhaustion.

Meanwhile, Jim still wasn't sure what had set Nick off. He figured it had something to do with Ian and Eric, but he'd never seen them do

15

anything to Nick before. *What could have happened?* he wondered as he stared over at Nick on the chair. Unexpectedly, he noticed Nick's eyes peer sideways, stopping to focus at the open space on the desk. Jim's eyes followed. *OH NO!* It immediately dawned on him what had happened: Ian and Eric had stolen Nick's jar of money.

"Those losers! Man, they make me so mad!" Jim steamed. Taking a deep breath, he turned back to Nick and put out his hand to him. Nick didn't respond. Jim assured him, "Don't worry. I'll get your money back. Those losers will not be allowed to come here again."

After spending a few more minutes in the chair, Nick got up, grabbed his delivery bag and walked over toward Jim, who was busy making phone calls. Nick wasn't sure exactly what was happening, but he could hear bits and pieces of the phone conversations. "… they were late for work … stole money from the center … bring the money back … not welcome here any more …"

Next Jim hung up the phone and turned to Nick, who was ready with his delivery bag over his shoulder. "Nick, you still wanna deliver your papers?"

Nick handed Jim a card that he was holding in his hand. It read "Deliver Papers" and had a picture of a boy carrying newspapers.

"Great, Nick! You're an awesome worker. Okay, about your money jar, I just talked with both of the boys' moms. I am sorry about what happened. Ian and Eric will bring your jar back this afternoon. After that, they will not be allowed at the community center."

Nick was feeling better at hearing what Jim had just arranged. He handed him the picture card again. *C'mon. Let's go!*

"Okay, okay, let me get my keys to lock up. It's a beautiful day for a paper route," said Jim.

Extra! Extra!

They headed out the door and into the neighborhood to deliver their newspapers. Jim had the delivery list detailing which house numbers were to receive papers, and he pointed at the driveways as they passed those houses. Nick pulled papers out of his bag and tossed them onto the driveways. When the last paper was thrown, they walked back to the community center to grab a soda and wait for the other teens to return from their routes.

When Nick's mom entered the center at the end of the day, Nick was busy playing a game and barely looked up. Noticing her enter, Jim approached Mrs. Hansen and explained, as best he could, the situation between Nick and the other teens earlier that morning.

Jim continued, "Mrs. Hansen, those boys will no longer be joining us here at the community center. This afternoon, they returned Nick's money, apologized to him and also deposited their earnings from today into Nick's jar. You should be proud of how hard Nick worked this summer! I am sure he has earned enough money for the shoes he wants."

"Thank you for handling this so quickly," Mrs. Hansen replied.

Jim interrupted Nick during his game, "Hey, Nick, show your mom the shoes you want." Nick looked up and smiled at his mom. Handing the money jar to Nick while pointing at the picture, Jim repeated, "Nick, show your mom the shoes you earned."

Nick took the jar and pointed at the advertisement. "Shoes," he said.

"Good job, Nicky. I'm so proud of you," said his mom. "Thank you, Jim. See you tomorrow. Movie Day, right?"

"Yes, see you tomorrow, Mrs. Hansen. High-five, Nick," he said putting his hand up.

In His Shoes

After returning the high-five, for a brief moment Nick paused and gazed directly into Jim's eyes, hard as it was for him, as if to say, "Thank you."

Jim appreciated the intense eye contact and said, "Great job, Nick."

"Great job, Nick," Nick repeated back as he and his mom headed to the car.

Holding tightly to the jar of money, Nick sat down in the passenger seat of the car. He wouldn't let go of the jar, so his mom buckled his seatbelt for him. Beaming with pride, he looked steadily at the picture of the shoes he had worked so hard to earn. "Shoes." Nick unscrewed the lid and reached into the jar. All the way home, his mom could hear the sound of coins clinking together as Nick sifted through them with his fingers. *My shoes*, he thought. *My shoes.*

POINTS TO PONDER ...

 Nick's parents easily could afford to buy him a new pair of shoes. Why do you think Nick's job coach had him earn money for shoes?

 Have you ever seen anyone take advantage of another person who couldn't defend himself? What could you do in a situation like that to help?

 Unfortunately, kids with autism are bullied quite often. What do you think makes them easy targets and how can you help prevent any child from being bullied?

 If a person is unable to speak using words, do you think that means he can't hear or understand you? Do you think he can communicate without using words? Can you think of some examples?

 How would you feel if people talked negatively about you directly in front of you and you couldn't respond?

Another Day,
Another Mall

"**N**icky! Get your shoes on. It's ten o'clock – time to go to the mall. It's new-shoe day!" Karen hollered up the stairwell.

New-shoe day. "Shoes," came Nick's voice from upstairs.

Nick hated going to the mall, but having a teenage girl in the family made the mall a permanent fixture in the Hansen family schedule. Nick liked spending time with Karen, even though they usually didn't enjoy the same activities. But it hadn't always been like this.

As children, they had fought a LOT. Karen resented all of the attention Nick received from his parents, but at the same time she'd felt guilty for being upset. Most of her elementary school years she had felt she was "on her own" since her parents were always busy finding therapies for Nick or handling medical insurance problems. Plus, Nick was always sneaking into her room and messing with her stuff. She even hung up signs that read "KEEP OUT!" and put padlocks on her bedroom door to stop him from entering. Also, Nick's behavior embarrassed Karen in front of her friends. For a long time, she wished she had a "normal" brother.

That was then!

As the kids matured into teens, they developed respect for each other and got along – most of the time, at least.

Karen was 17, a senior in high school, and Nick was 13. Karen's favorite hobby was spending time with her girlfriends, texting friends and talking on the phone with boys. Nick preferred to be alone listening to his iPod at the park or watching action adventure movies. He didn't understand the social stuff in life. It was tricky for him. It was like everyone else had this secret rule book telling you how to act with other people, but no one shared it with him. Plus, people always assumed he knew how they felt by the expressions on their faces or the way they moved or turned their bodies. He just didn't get it and always felt like he was missing something.

"Nicky, let's go! Remember, shoes!" Karen called again up the stairs.

Hearing that, Nick got so excited that he practically tripped down the stairs with his shoes half-way on. Karen helped him get his shoes on properly, ran a comb through his hair and straightened his shirt. Then she grabbed his communication book in one hand and jiggled the car keys in front of him with the other. "It's shoe time, bro. Let's go!" she said as they walked out the front door.

Another Day, Another Mall

Nick smiled fiercely and giggled, envisioning himself sitting in the front seat while Karen drove, "YES!!" Then he turned and ran back inside to get his favorite CDs.

Twisted by the whirlwind of her brother, Karen asked, "Where are you going now?"

"YES!" He grabbed his CD case off the kitchen table and practically flew back out the front door, spinning Karen in the other direction. For Nick, riding with Karen was fun. It wasn't like riding with his mom, who played music from the '80s that put him to sleep half the time. If he had to listen to REO Speedwagon one more time, he thought he might throw up! *Not today!* Nick was going to be in charge of selecting the music for the ride to the mall. He flipped opened his communication book and pulled out a card that showed a picture of a CD. Next he handed it to Karen.

"Yes, Nick, you can play your music," she answered.

He smiled. Karen was cool. Nick had heard everyone talk about how cool she was. He wasn't even sure exactly what "cool" meant, but he knew it was a good thing by the way other kids talked. It was amazing what things people said right in front of Nick. "Yah, Nick, like, he's cool in a weird, freaky sort of way...," they'd say right within earshot. Just because he didn't respond, they somehow thought he didn't hear them. It's as if he was invisible. He figured that they weren't trying to be cruel, but sometimes the things they said hurt his feelings.

He also heard kids talking about his clothes a lot, "Why does he wear those same shorts every day?"

Why not? he wondered. *I like them.*

In His Shoes

One time, a girl giggled, walked up to him and said, "Ha, Nick, your shirt is so *yesterday*."

Huh? What the heck does that mean? he wondered. Nick didn't care much about what he wore as long as it was comfortable.

When they arrived at the mall, *shoes, shoes, shoes, shoes* was the mantra Nick repeated in his head as he galloped from the car across the parking lot. Karen practically fell out of her flip flops trying to keep up.

As they walked through the food court entrance, all of Nick's senses were on high alert. Smelling the nauseating combination of each and every food item all at once, he wondered, *how can so many yummy foods smell so nasty when all mixed together? I don't get it.* Mind-numbing music blaring from the mall speakers clashed with the noise of the elevators moving up and down while the clickety-clack of hundreds of shoes echoed as they hit the marble floor.

What is that itchy thing on my neck? He scrunched his shoulders trying to adjust the tag on his shirt. At the same time, he felt his sock sink deeper into his shoe, causing an uncomfortable lump under his foot with every step he took, *ugh!* Following his sister, with his eyes turned down to avoid eye contact with others, the glare reflecting onto the floor from the lights above was becoming painful to his eyes. He pulled his sunglasses from his shirt pocket and put them on.

Trying to filter all these sensations out, it was hard for him to concentrate on what his sister was saying "… and then, like, Julie told me that she got totally burned at the beach yesterday. I told her to use sunscreen, but she said it's not even sunny – it's overcast. – Duh! So now she can't go to the pool with us tomorrow. So, I told her, try Aloe Vera gel and then she's, like …"

Another Day, Another Mall

He covered his ears tightly to block out the distracting noises from the mall, which were clashing with his sister's boring conversation. He tried to concentrate visually on what was in front of him.

As he walked around the mall, Nick recognized some of the logos advertising surfer-style clothing. *Hey, Jim showed me that,* he remembered as he thought back to the two of them looking through magazines at the community center.

Jim had said, "Check out this, Nick. These board shorts are SWEEEEET!"

Hmmm – sweet? Nick had wondered, *Who would taste their shorts?*

As they continued walking toward the shoe store, Karen said, "Nick, next time we go to the mall, I'll help you find some new clothes for school. You'll be the coolest-looking seventh grader on campus. And don't worry – no itchy tags or scratchy fabrics. I've got your number, bro."

He scrunched his eyes and wondered, *Huh? What number does she have of mine? Ugh, she's planning another trip to the mall.*

They finally arrived at the shoe store. As they entered, Nick was so excited that he began practically dancing around. Held tightly in his hand, he looked at the worn and tattered advertisement showing the shoes he wanted to buy. His eyes darted around as he compared the picture he had brought to each pair of shoes, looking for a perfect match. He could scan visually with awesome speed.

In His Shoes

After Karen directed him to the section with athletic shoes, he quickly found the exact match. "Shoes. SAME!" Karen helped him find his size, and he tried them on. *Awesome,* he thought, staring at his feet. Karen even let him wear the new shoes out of the store. Mission accomplished! *Let's go home.* Nick saw no other purpose to be at the mall.

"Okay, kiddo, let's head out," said Karen generously, knowing that the mall was not Nick's favorite place. "Wanna get something in the food court or go straight home?"

"Home."

"Sure you don't want a slice of pizza? It's on me!"

Huh? "Home," repeated Nick.

"Alrighty then; home it is, Nick."

As they headed toward the exit, Nick was distracted by the noises in the food court: stir fry sizzling on the grill, more annoying music and hundreds of conversations going on at the same time all around them. It was like having a bunch of TVs on, all broadcasting different channels at a deafening volume. Suddenly he stopped and began to rock back and forth, covering his ears to block out the sounds. The motion made him feel more at ease.

Just then Cindy, one of Karen's friends, ran up and grabbed him from behind. Caught off guard, Nick was not ready to accept that jolt of energy pulsing through his body. He balled up his fists to protect himself from what he perceived as a threat. As he turned around, he recognized Cindy, but it was too late.

Karen caught his fist just in time, "No! Nick, it's just Cindy." He knew Cindy and liked her a lot, but she had frightened him.

Another Day, Another Mall

Karen explained, "Cindy, please don't sneak up on Nick. It really scares him."

Cindy was embarrassed, "Geez, sorry, Nick." Then she started talking to him really loudly, rattling off so many words so fast that he was still processing the first two – "Hey, Nick" – when she finished with something that sounded like a question.

Realizing it was his turn to respond, but not sure what to say, Nick just repeated, "Hey, Nick" back to her.

Cindy giggled, "Nick, you are, like, so funny! I love it when you do that!"

Karen rolled her eyes and shook her head.

While Cindy was gushing out hundreds of words to Karen, Nick soon lost interest and stared off toward the food court at the lady wearing the funny beanie hat. *Lemons.* She appeared to be making a pool full of lemonade. Through the clear glass container, he watched the lemons and ice sloshing up and down, over and over again. That repetitive wavy motion helped him feel more relaxed. "Home."

Then as quickly as she had arrived, Cindy ran off, yelling over her shoulder, "Later, Nick. I like your new shoes! They're so cool!"

Smiling nervously, he looked down at his "cool" new shoes. *Cool. Shoes.*

POINTS TO PONDER ...

 How do you think it might feel to be Nick's sister? Do you think she ever feels embarrassed or gets frustrated with Nick? What types of things might make her feel proud to be his sister?

 Have you ever tried to communicate or interact with a friend's brother or sister who had a disability? How did you feel? How did your friend's sibling react?

 When Cindy greeted Nick and he simply mimicked her greeting back, this is known as "echolalia." Many people with autism use this form of communication. Why do you think they repeat back the greeting as opposed to replying back more naturally? Do you think it could be frustrating for someone speaking with a person who has autism to just have phrases repeated back instead of a typical conversation? How might you help someone with autism respond?

 People with autism sometimes have "sensory issues" (sensitivity to taste, vision, touch, hearing and smell). Do you ever experience problems or challenges with any of your senses? Do you have clothing that you don't like because it feels itchy or tight? Are there noises or smells that bother you sometimes?

 When you have a conversation, you probably *filter out* other sounds in the room to concentrate on the other person's voice. How do you think the conversation would go if you constantly heard *all* of the other distracting noises at the same volume as the conversation? Would you find it hard to focus?

Beach Day ...
Hurray!

With the end of summer approaching, the Hansen family headed to the beach for one last day of ocean fun. Each of them loved the beach, but for different reasons. Nick's dad enjoyed walking with Nick along the tide pools, inspecting little creatures and finding living treasures to show him. Nick's mom looked forward to building sandcastles and relaxing under the umbrella with her favorite summer books. Karen's "job" was to work on her tan and swim with her little brother. For Nick, the entire experience was awesome. The beach was like a second home to him. At the ocean, he was comfortable and felt like he was part of a very special world.

In His Shoes

The way the family car was crammed with coolers, umbrellas, boogie boards, sand toys and towels, it looked like they were going to be staying at the beach for a month instead of just one day. Arriving before most of the tourists had even crawled out of bed for their first cup of coffee, the Hansens got a front parking spot. With quarters in his hand, Nick virtually bounced out of the car. "Clink, Tick Tick Tick, Clink, Tick Tick Tick …" Nick's job was to fill the parking meter with quarters. Next, everyone grabbed stuff out of the car, as mom led the way toward an area near the lifeguard stand. On some trips, they would only spend a few hours at the beach if Nick became irritable, but they usually stayed the entire day. The end-of-the-summer beach trip was a tradition they never skipped.

Mr. Hansen was finishing slathering more sunscreen on Nick when Mrs. Hansen called, "Come on, Nicky! It's sandcastle time."

Nick slipped away from dad, grabbed his super-deluxe sandcastle building kit and trotted off towards his mom. His aunt had sent him the kit for his birthday. It was one of his favorite gifts. His dad caught up with him and tossed a sun visor on his head – he was now totally ready for a day in the sun.

Joining his mom at the edge of the wet sand, the two of them started, as always, by digging a huge moat around the castle construction zone. Mom's famous line was, "If you don't have a solid moat, your castle will float." She always said this just as they started building.

Beach Day ... Hurray!

Nick dropped the buckets nearby and dug his hand into the wet sand. Spreading the sand granules between his fingers, he looked at the sand intensely. *Feels interesting.*

Noticing that Nick was getting mesmerized by the sand, his mom called, "Hey Nicky, come on. Let's get going on the castle!"

As if snapping out of a trance, Nick got up and joined her.

In his younger years, Nick was fascinated watching the dry sand filter through the sand-wheels. It was as if he saw and counted each grain of sand. If given the chance, he would watch for hours as each speck went through the wheel and hit the beach, gradually creating a small pile.

When Nick was in preschool, his therapist used to take him to the beach to play with the sand and learn skills such as taking turns and imitating. Now he was more of a junior engineer in the sandcastle department, working with the senior engineer, his mom.

When they were done with their masterpiece, Karen ran up with the camera, "Say cheese!" With an awkward smile and eyes looking away from the camera, Nick knew that it was time for the traditional sandcastle photo. "Wow, Team Hansen, that's one of your best creations yet! Look, Nick," Karen said handing him the camera.

Nick looked at the digital photo displayed on the camera, "Castle."

"That's right, castle! Ready to swim, Nick?" Karen asked, handing the camera to her dad. Then she put out her hand for Nick, who grabbed it and pulled her to the water's edge.

Mrs. Hansen smiled and turned happily to her husband, "Karen sure has matured. Look how good she is with Nick now."

"I remember just a few years ago when she wouldn't even be seen with him at the beach. She would have put her beach towel near the next lifeguard tower," her husband nodded.

"Honey, our babies are growing up!" They both smiled.

"Yes, they are."

Brrrrr, Nick thought as the tiny waves lapped onto his toes, tickling him with the freezing-cold water. Once his toes were used to it, he and Karen waded out into knee-high water and waited for a medium-sized wave to crash at their bellies. Nick felt comfortable in the ocean as the water embraced his body. Being at the beach was a break from many of the sensory issues that challenged him on a daily basis. He enjoyed the sensations he experienced at the beach: the sound of the waves crashing, the feel of sand in his toes and the ocean breeze blowing his hair under the warm sunshine.

He looked back at the lifeguard tower at the warning flag. *Green.* "Green."

"That's right, Nick. The lifeguard flag is green. It's safe for swimming. Wanna hit the waves?" Karen prompted.

"Hit the waves!" Nick repeated giggling. He had learned what those words meant and had memorized them. He tugged Karen's arm so hard he practically yanked it out of the socket while dragging her further into the waves. Karen let Nick judge how far out they went. Even though his style was not the most graceful, he was a strong swimmer. Sometimes the waves would go high and crash over his head. He had learned to hold his breath and close his eyes when this happened. Once in a while, the salt water would rush up into his nose. *Yuck!* Aside from that, he loved the feeling of the waves crashing over him and would play in the waves for hours.

"Hey, Nick, wanna catch a wave on the boogie board?" Karen called.

A big smile lit up Nick's face as he repeated, "boogie board, boogie board, boogie board ..." until Karen brought it to him.

Karen helped Nick steady himself up onto the boogie board. He loved the feeling of being on the board as it glided on top of the water. Gentle waves lapped over his board tickling his body with each chilly embrace. By next summer, he would most likely be able to boogie board without Karen's help. For a moment, the water was calm and peaceful.

As he sat on the board waiting for the next swell, Nick's mind drifted back to the previous summer when his cousin had taken him to Surfers Healing Camp – a camp created to provide kids with autism the unique experience of surfing. His cousin had prepared him months in advance by sharing surfing magazines, watching DVDs and even occasionally going to the beach to observe real surfers in action. Finally, his surf day arrived! As his cousin pulled into the beach parking lot, Nick practically galloped out of the car twirling the string on his swim trunks in nervous anticipation.

Arriving at the beach, they were greeted by a volunteer who soon took Nick toward the water's edge. Right away, he was introduced to Austin, his personal surfing coach. Austin quickly gained Nick's trust as he talked with Nick about various ocean animals. Then he showed Nick how to stand on the board with the proper positioning. At last! It was time to surf. Austin paddled Nick out into the ocean, and they surfed tandem for several waves. What a blast! Recognizing Nick was comfortable in the ocean, Austin decided to let him try surfing on his own. Surfing solo – what a thrill! While waiting for his last wave, a strange shape formed

In His Shoes

nearby on the water, catching Nick's attention. Unexpectedly, he noticed several dolphins gently gliding in and out of the water looking his direction. It was like they were swimming by to say, "Hey, bud. Welcome to our world!"

A splash of water in Nick's face jolted him back to the present time. "Hello?! Earth to Nick, are you with me?" Karen teased to get his attention. He giggled and grabbed tighter to the boogie board. Together, they caught the next wave. Karen and Nick continued to boogie board catching wave after wave.

Suddenly, their fun was interrupted by their mom calling, "LUNCH TIME!" Karen could see her mom waving her arms at them. She waved back.

Nick's stomach rumbled when Karen mentioned that it was time for lunch. Soon they joined their parents for a delicious picnic lunch. Nick quickly ate his triangular cuts of turkey sandwich, careful not to get sand on them. He hated the way sand gritted between his teeth when it got on his food. He kept thinking in his head, *Sand Witch, Sand Witch ... I hate sand in my sandwich!* At that thought, he began giggling. Everyone else wondered what was so funny, but without knowing for sure, they laughed along with him.

After finishing his last triangle, Nick reached into the bag of Bugle snacks. Their cone shape reminded him of fingernails. He put one on each finger like scary fingernails and then ate them one by one from each fingertip.

"Drink your water, kids. You don't want to get dehydrated," their mom cautioned.

Nick took a gulp of water just as a seagull flew past his towel. He loved watching the seagulls, which remained close while he ate.

The birds hovered in place over his family – waiting and watching. He enjoyed listening to their screechy noise. Picturing the seagulls from *Finding Nemo*, Nick listened to them and tried to imagine them screaming, "Mine! Mine! Mine!" When he tossed a few Bugles into the sand nearby, with a flutter of wings, the seagulls dive bombed for the snacks. Nick's hands flapped in delight. As they slowly walked up to him and tilted their heads, it was as if the seagulls were holding a conversation with him. Nick was mesmerized until Karen snapped him out of it.

"Nick, stop attracting those stupid seagulls! They're so obnoxious!" she whined.

"Oh, Karen, they aren't hurting anything. Right, Nick?" Mr. Hansen intervened.

Nick thought of the seagulls as his friends. They enjoyed his company and they were always dependable – especially for a lunch date.

After a huge circle of seagulls surrounded the family, Nick's mom finally shooed them away, "Enough! Get out of here you nasty seagulls." The whooshing sound of all the wings flapping away in symphony excited Nick so much that he got up and began bouncing up and down, flapping his own hands rapidly. He looked ready to take off flying with them.

"Kids, are you ready for the tide pools?" asked Mr. Hansen.

"Tide pools," Nick repeated as he hurried to put on his sandals.

"Not today, Dad. Gotta work on my tan. Senior year, ya know," laughed Karen.

"Karen, honey, make sure you put on more sunscreen. Remember what happened to Julie last week," warned her mom.

"Yah, you mean Julie, the lobster girl?"

Nick headed off with his dad toward the rocky reef area. He knew that there were tiny critters living all over the reef and, therefore, tried to walk cautiously on the rocks. He'd been exploring tide pools with his dad since he was a toddler. Back then, his dad would carry him on his shoulders and show him the favorite hiding places of sea urchins, sea anemones, hermit crabs and sea slugs. It was amazing how many different animals lived in this tide pool zone. For years, Nick was so obsessed with the tide pools that he carried around books and flash cards related to tide pools. He even slept with a stuffed sea star. Back then he dreamed of being an oceanographer, but he had pretty much given up that dream.

"Don't forget, Nick. We can touch, but we gotta put them back where we find them. Back to their home," his dad reminded him.

Home. This was their home. Nick understood, because he liked the comfort of his home, too.

One thing that had baffled Nick all these years was why the tide pools were visible sometimes, but at other times they were covered with water. He remembered his dad had mentioned something about the pull of the sun and the moon on the earth, but he didn't fully understand what his dad meant. He wanted to ask more about it. This was just one of the hundreds of questions that he wished he could ask his dad. Sometimes, not being able to talk about things like that really sucked.

Beach Day ... Hurray!

After a while Nick's mom approached, interrupting their exploring. "HEY! Guys! Time to pack up. The parking meter is going to run out of time soon!"

When her mom returned to the blanket, Karen rolled over and reminded her, "Mom, be sure we don't forget the sandcastle demolition crew."

Karen got up and stretched. As Nick and their dad approached, she grabbed the camera out of her mom's bag and said, "Nicky, it's show time. Jump the castle! Ready, set ..."

"GO!" Nick said as he took a flying leap right into the castle. Then he wiggled his body all over and started making patterns that looked like sand angels.

Karen pointed the camera and snapped away. Finally, Nick, the sand monster, rose from the ruins of the formerly majestic castle. His mom and dad laughed as he shook off the loose sand.

"It's off to the showers with you, Sir Nicholas!" teased his mom. She thought she heard Nick groan in response.

As they drove out of the parking lot, Nick looked out the window at the sun, which was beginning to set over the ocean. *Beautiful.* He wiggled his toes and felt the grains of sand gritting between them. Smiling, he thought back on yet another wonderful day at the beach.

POINTS TO PONDER ...

 The Hansens' day at the beach sounded fun. Do you like going to the beach? What do you like to do at the beach?

 Think about your senses (sight, hearing, touch, taste and smell). What kind of sensory experiences do you like at the beach? What kind of sensory experiences do you not like at the beach?

 Are there other activities that you enjoy at the beach that you think Nick might like to try?

 Imagine you were at the beach the same day as the Hansen family. Are there any activities that Nick likes that you might be interested in? How would you approach him to join in on those activities?

End of Summer, What a Bummer

The end of summer was always a challenge for Nick since it meant a new school year would be starting and all the changes that would bring. This year not only was he transitioning to middle school, he would also have a new teacher, a new schedule and new aides. Changes to routines tended to increase Nick's stress levels. He liked to know what to expect and when to expect it.

A few days before school started, Nick's mom and dad helped him adjust by taking him to see his new classroom. They called ahead to make sure his new teacher, Miss Flowers, would be available so they could be introduced. Pacing back and forth in the school parking lot with his hands fluttering towards his face, it was obvious that Nick was a bit nervous. "It'll be fine, Nick. You'll see," his dad reassured him. He had toured the campus during an orientation in the spring, but school was in session then so they never actually went into any of the classrooms.

At first Nick was hesitant to enter the classroom. It seemed so different from those at his elementary school. Prior to this year, Nick had attended the same school since he was 3 years old. His mom held his hand and nudged him a bit. *I'm scared. This is different.* Finally, Nick entered the room, but he began to make odd noises. Although he recognized some of the visual reminders and schedules around the room, he didn't see many of the fun posters he remembered from elementary school. His eyes darted around the room and suddenly stopped at a shelf containing a collection of shining seashells. He cautiously moved toward them to get a closer look.

A little farther into the room, they could see a lady standing on a chair stapling photos to a wall. Hearing them, she turned around and smiled brightly. "Well, Nicholas Hansen, it's so good to finally meet you." She recognized him from the picture in his file. "Nick, how are you?" she said, stepping off the chair and putting out her hand toward him.

Nick reached out, gently touched her hand and repeated, "How are you?" *She seems nice. Hmm, Miss Flowers smells like a flower. That's funny. Smells like sweet peas.* He looked up at his mom, trying to convey the message in his head. *Hey, mom, she smells like you!* The only word spoken was, "Flowers."

"Miss Flowers, that's right, Nick," replied Miss Flowers kindly.

"Hello, Mr. and Mrs. Hansen. Come on in. Please feel free to explore the classroom. Here is Nick's desk and his new keyboard that we discussed in his last IEP meeting," Miss Flowers said holding out a shiny new communication keyboard to Nick's dad. He sat down and began testing it out.

End of Summer, What a Bummer

"Since learning a keyboard is one of his new goals, his aides and the speech therapist will begin assisting him with it during school," explained Miss Flowers. "We will also continue to utilize his school communication book. His teacher from last year sent it over to me with his files."

Noticing that Nick was looking intently at the seashell collection, Miss Flowers called, "Nick, come over here, please. I'd like to show you the students who will be in our class." Mrs. Hansen guided him over to the photo wall. "This is Miguel … this is Jacob … this is Riley … this is Eva …" Miss Flowers continued as Nick recognized the photos of Miguel, Riley and Eva, whom he knew from his sixth-grade class. Seeing some familiar faces made him smile.

"CLICK."

"Perfect, Nick – a beautiful smile!" Miss Flowers said as she snapped a photo of him. "Fabulous! We'll use this photo for visual aids in the classroom – like Nick's desk, his backpack, his grooming supplies … oh, and of course, our class photo wall."

Nick's dad returned the keyboard to Miss Flowers and noticed that Nick was already back at the other side of the room busily organizing the seashells by size. "Well, we'd better get going, son." He gently helped Nick put the last shell down and said, "Time to go home, Nick."

"Home," replied Nick.

"Thank you for showing us around," said Mrs. Hansen.

Miss Flowers walked up to the three of them and reached her hand out to Nick. "Welcome to middle school. I'll see you next week, Nick."

"Next week, Nick," Nick echoed and touched her hand gently.

"Goodbye, Miss Flowers. Enjoy your last week of summer," Nick's mom said as they headed out the door for home.

Later that weekend, while Nick's mom and sister were helping him prepare for his first day of school, he paced around the room. It looked as though he wasn't paying any attention, but he was actually listening intently.

Karen patiently explained, "Nicholas, middle school is different in so many ways. Recess will be called break. And there's no play-ground. Sorry bud, no swings or slides." She grabbed his commu-nication book. "Kids in middle school like to hang out," she said showing him a new picture of a group of kids standing around.

Unless they were going to be talking about his favorite new CD, Nick thought, *Booooring!*

Karen also packed him a baggie of his favorite snack, Cheetos, and marked them with his name. She snuck him a few in the process. "This bag is for your lunch. That other baggie, marked 'friends,' is to share with other students." She then pointed at the Cheetos bag marked "friends" and the picture of kids hanging out. "You might meet some new friends if you share your extra Cheetos with other students." She continued, "They might even share some of their snacks with you."

"Snacks," Nick smiled. *That sounds good.* "Mmmmm."

Overhearing the discussion, Nick's mom interrupted. "That's true. Sometimes the way to a friend's heart is through his stomach." *Ugh. Oops – that's an idiom.* She temporarily forgot that using idioms like that with Nick usually didn't work very well since he tended to think of things literally.

Nick didn't understand what a friend's heart and stomach had to do with sharing snacks. The picture that idea created in his mind totally confused him. He reached for his communication book and flipped through it. When he found the page with the pictures of emotions, he scanned them *happy, sad, sick ... Confused, that's it.* He pulled it out of the book, showed his mom and said, "Confused."

"Ooops. Sorry, Nick. I meant that if you share your snacks, it might help you meet some new kids at school. Let me show you."

From the pocket of his communication book, his mom pulled out a larger laminated index card that had two little squares of Velcro attached next to each other. Grabbing two picture cards from Nick's book, she attached the picture of *snacks* on the left and the picture of *friends* on the right. Then, with a marker, she drew an equal sign in between the two picture cards. Through pictures, it showed *snacks* equals *friends*.

"Is that better?" she asked Nick. That little visual tool made it easier for him to understand how the Cheetos related to making friends. He knew he liked it when people offered him snacks. While sneaking another Cheeto, he considered this idea and watched as his mom wrote a note.

His mom attached the note to the snack bag as a reminder to Nick's aide to encourage him to sit with other students at break and to assist Nick in offering them some Cheetos. Fortunately, Nick was not on a special diet (some children with autism are) and could choose to eat whatever the other kids offered. He was nervous, but was curious to find out exactly what this "hanging out" was.

Next Nick's mom packed up all his school supplies in his new backpack. "No more Sponge Bob! According to your sister, you *have* to *have* a Jansport backpack this year."

Nick wondered, *Hmmm. What's wrong with Sponge Bob?* Oh well, as long as he could put his iPod in the backpack, he didn't really care.

His mom made new picture cards on the computer to represent the classes Nick would be taking at school. Nick attended a self-contained class that supported kids with autism. It served as his homeroom. Throughout the day, he would go back and forth between this room and other classes (like art, computers and P.E.) for different subject periods. He was excited about taking the computer class. He had chosen this as an elective during registration.

Finally, unlacing Nick's new shoes, his mom looped the laces through a metal identification tag. The tag showed Nick's name, address and phone number, and also noted "autism and nonverbal." Nick carried an I.D. card in his wallet, but sometimes when he was anxious, he forgot to pull it out if someone asked his name. This I.D. tag might help him better communicate his information in an emergency or if he was anxious. Sometimes items like this became his voice when he was unable to speak. It was an additional safety measure the family took when Nick ventured out into the community.

As they were finishing up, Mrs. Hansen commented, "Okay Nick, one more day until middle school!" She was trying to be cheerful, but there was a glint of moisture in her eyes. "Middle school," she repeated with a sigh, blinking hard to try to hold back her tears.

"Middle school," Nick echoed as he looked down at his name on his shiny ID tag on his new school shoes. "Middle school."

POINTS TO PONDER ...

- If you were Nick's sister, what is some advice you would give him while he got ready to transition (change over) from elementary to middle school? What sort of pictures would you use to visually describe some of your advice?

- What are ways that Nick might meet people at middle school?

- Are there any activities or groups at your school that you think Nick might enjoy? How could you welcome or invite someone like Nick to these activities or groups?

- What classes at your school do you think Nick might like? How could other kids be supportive of him in those classes? Have you ever been in a class with a student who faced challenges similar to Nick's? What are some examples of how the kids interacted with that student? What are some examples of how that student positively impacted the class?

Back-to-School Blues

On the morning of the first day of school, Nick's mom waited with him in front of their house for the school bus to arrive. He stood rocking back and forth in a motion that comforted him. Covering one ear with his hand, he shut out some of the noise from the bus as it turned the corner and pulled up.

Nick thought, *YES! It's bus #11!* He remembered that Jon, his favorite bus driver, was usually the driver of bus #11. Plus, 11 was his favorite number – so perfectly aligned. *Yes!* "Bus 11," he thought out loud.

"Yes, honey. It's bus number 11. Nick, give me a hug goodbye," his mom said, opening her arms for him. "Bye, honey. I love you."

In His Shoes

Nick let his mom hug him and said, "BaBye," as he walked toward the bus.

Opening the door, Jon smiled, "Hey there, Nick!"

Nick repeated, "Hey there, Nick!" as he climbed on board.

"Jon."

"Jon," Nick repeated with a smile, looking at the driver.

Once on the bus, Nick turned left and sat down by the window in the second row, the same seat he always chose. Then he opened his backpack and took out his iPod. He put on his headphones and turned on his music to block out some of the sounds that irritated him on the bus. As the bus shifted gears to take off, Nick stared out the window. He saw his mom quickly wipe a tear from her eye. *Mom is sad.* Rumbling, the bus drove off.

There were seven other students assigned to ride on this morning bus route. Nick was the first on, so his ride felt like it lasted forever. As other students got on the bus, Nick appeared to be in his own little world. He didn't seem to notice or acknowledge any of them. Nor did any of them strike up a conversation with him or with each other. This bus ride definitely wasn't a social occasion for these kids. It was merely how they got to school each day.

As the bus pulled into the school driveway forty minutes later, Nick saw through the window a familiar person on the sidewalk. "Kate," he whispered. *Awesome.* He was happy to recognize, waiting for him at the bus stop area, one of his favorite aides from several years prior. "Kate."

As Nick exited the bus, Kate approached, smiling brightly. "Well, Nicholas Hansen, how have you been? I've missed you!" She held out her hand and patiently waited for his response.

Nick reached out to touch her hand gently and said, "Kate."

Kate handed him a map of the campus. "Let's take a look at this," she suggested as they moved to the side out of the flow of students.

"After break today, we are going to take a tour of the school and get to know the campus better. We'll put a copy of this map in your binder, too. Okay, we'd better get to class."

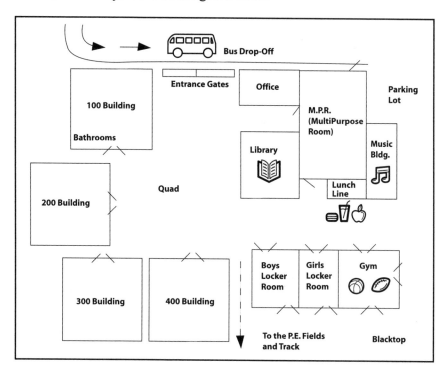

Nick took Kate's hand, and they began walking to class. Kate gently removed Nick's hand from hers and said, "Nick we're in middle school now. Sorry, no hand holding, buddy." Then she put her hand gently on his shoulder to let him know she was there to help guide him to class. He felt more secure. Although his anxiety was increasing, so far things were going okay, and middle school might not be as scary as he had imagined.

In His Shoes

As they passed through the school gates, the noise level increased almost immediately. The first few days of school were always especially hectic as new students scurried about trying to find their classes and reunite with old friends. Weaving in and out among frenzied teens, Kate and Nick made their way across the quad to the 400 Building. Nick began feeling more anxious. There were so many students rushing every which way, and the noise was becoming unbearable. It reminded Nick of how he felt when he was at the train station with his dad during afternoon rush hour. He felt he was in the middle of a tornado. His brain was receiving too much information from all around – like a computer being overloaded with data all at once. *Too loud. Slow down. People are touching me. I need a break.*

Kate could sense Nick's anxiety increasing. Her goal was to get him from the bus to the classroom as quickly as possible while also trying to protect him from getting overly stressed out. *Whew! Just in time!* She opened the door to the building, and the noise level reduced dramatically. "Nick, here's the class. Right in here, room 403," she said pointing as she directed him into his classroom. "Nick, the first few days of school are always a little crazy. It will get better as the kids figure out their schedules," she added reassuringly.

As they entered the room, the noise level decreased even more. Even though Nick had visited the classroom the week before, being there without his parents and taking in all the sights, smells and sounds of the class was too much for him to handle all at once. He began to flap his hands and rock front and back, saying over and over "Thank you for your hospitality, but we really have to go. Thank you for your hospitality, but we really have to go ..." a line from the movie *Chronicles of Narnia*. It helped calm him.

Kate, let's go. I'm not comfortable here. "Thank you for your hospitality, but we really have to go..."

Other students in the class were also nervous and anxious. Across the aisle, Eva was sitting at her desk quietly. "Excuse me. Was there a big yellow bird on this plane? Excuse me. Was there a big yellow bird on this plane? ..." she kept repeating over and over as she looked at a book about ice skating. In the meantime, Riley was jumping on a small trampoline while his aide counted with him from one to one hundred.

Nick's rocking quickly appeared more agitated than soothing – a sign that his anxiety was escalating. Flipping open his communication book on his desk, Kate handed him a yellow card marked "BREAK" and guided him to the designated quiet area in the classroom. From working with Nick in the past, she remembered that offering deep pressure to his head, by squeezing it firmly and evenly, had a calming effect on him.

"Want pressure, Nick?" Kate asked as she put her hands out in front of him.

"Pressure, please," he responded, taking her hands to show it was okay. Kate began applying deep and steady pressure just above his ears.

Ahhhhhh, much better, he thought, reaching out for Kate's hands to do it again.

Soon he appeared more relaxed, so Kate suggested, "Ready for school?"

Looking up, Nick was excited to see a brand-new communication keyboard on his desk and headed over there right away. While Kate went to put her purse away, he sat down and turned on the keyboard. *This looks like my keyboard at home.* He slowly typed "N-I-C-H-O-L-A-S" and looked up. He saw some students he recognized and also some students he had never met.

"Okay, students, please sit down," Miss Flowers announced as she pointed on the board to a large picture of a student sitting in a chair. Some students responded immediately, others needed a reminder from an aide. Addressing both the students and the aides, Miss Flowers continued, "The Peer-Assisted Learning kids, better known as PALs, will be coming in later today to meet everyone." She pointed to "PALs" written on the board next to a large photo of kids wearing purple shirts marked "PALs." "They will be joining our class for games Mondays and Wednesdays during seventh period. They are looking forward to meeting all of you."

Before school got out in June, many students had applied for the PAL program after getting their teachers' recommendations. During lunch Miss Flowers would be meeting with the students who had been selected as PALs to explain some of the unique qualities and challenges of kids with autism. She would also discuss positive ways for them to interact with her students.

Nick soon tuned out Miss Flowers, concentrating on his new desk instead. A visual thinker, he quickly noticed his schedule on the desk. *Computers, YES!* He easily understood the pictures and also recognized many of the words connected with them. Not many people realized that Nick could read and comprehend a lot of words.

When his sister was in elementary school, she used to play "school" with Nick a lot. "Come on, Nick," Karen would say, "Time for spelling." She would write all of her spelling words on a dry-erase board and spell them out to him while reciting the vocabulary definitions. She also used to read aloud to Nick many of her chapter books. His favorites were the books in the *Harry Potter* series. With few classroom distractions during their game of school, Nick had learned a lot. Sometimes he paced around the room like a restless coyote appearing not to pay attention, but Karen just kept on teaching. Karen never knew how much Nick learned from her, but Nick knew. He was proud that this new teacher was finally putting written words next to the pictures on his schedule.

Here is what his schedule looked like for the first day of school:

Nick's Schedule – Monday

8:00-8:40		1st Period – Read a Book/Independent Work	☐
8:45-9:25		2nd Period – Computer Lab (Ms. Grimm's Lab – Room 205)	☐
9:30-10:10		3rd Period – Speech (Mrs. Carter's Office – Room 101)	☐
10:10-10:30		Break	☐
10:35-11:15		4th Period – Art (Miss Smith's Class – Room 401)	☐
11:20-12:00		5th Period – Deskwork & Goals	☐
12:00-12:35		Lunch	☐
12:40-1:20		6th Period – P.E. (Mr. Glenn's Class – in the gym)	☐
1:25-2:05		7th Period – Sensory/PALs/Games	☐
2:10		Pack up Backpack and Walk to Bus	☐

In His Shoes

As he looked at the first item on his schedule, Nick was happy to see "read a book." He picked up the erasable marker on his desk and checked off the first box. "READ A BOOK," he said with a gravelly voice. He loved looking through books and could read some. Peering out of the corner of his eyes, he searched the classroom for books. Nick had awesome peripheral vision since he used it often while avoiding eye contact with others. He saw a poster with "books" written on it and a picture of a bookshelf.

Kate watched Nick as he checked off "READ A BOOK." "Super, Nick. Go ahead. Get a book," she encouraged him.

Nick walked over to the bookshelf and was fascinated by the selection. "Basketball." He was even more excited to find his favorite book about NBA basketball players. He loved to look at the awesome sneakers the players wore. Holding the book, he looked down at his own shoes and then, without looking up, glanced around the room at his classmates' feet. He couldn't help but giggle out loud when he saw Riley wearing the exact same shoes as he did. "Same." Nick tapped his shoes twice with his fingers to acknowledge his new shoes to Riley.

POINTS TO PONDER ...

 There are a lot of visual reminders in Nick's classroom. What sort of visual reminders are used in your classroom? Do your teachers use any images to help you with your classroom activities?

 What about at home? Are there any visuals that help you throughout the day?

 When you enter a new situation (for example, a new classroom, new soccer team or a move to a new town), do you ever feel anxious, worried or stressed out? What do you do to help calm yourself?

 What are some ways Nick copes with stress and anxiety?

 It appears that Nick and his classmates find it difficult to interact or socialize with each other. What could an aide, a teacher or another student do to encourage interaction among the kids? Why do you think it might be important for these students to interact with other students at the school?

Life in the Fast Lane

Middle school P.E. was going to be another big adjustment for Nick. In August, during registration, his mother had purchased two P.E. uniforms for him. Nick used a permanent marker to write his last name on the shirts and shorts. After removing the tiny stitching from all the tags and washing the uniforms several times to soften the fabric so it would not be so itchy to Nick's sensitive skin, she pulled them out of the warm dryer and said, "Ooooh, so soft, Nick. It's just how you like 'em. Here."

Nick reached over and rubbed his hands on the warm, soft fabric. *Ahhhhh, nice.* He grabbed the pile and ran up to his room to try them on right away. He loved them so much that he ended up wearing the P.E. clothes to bed every night after that. Mrs. Hansen was glad she had bought two pairs so that he could keep the extra set at home.

In His Shoes

In elementary school, P.E. had been scheduled only twice each week. Now Nick would be participating in P.E. every day. On the first day of school, after returning to the classroom a bit early from lunch, Kate said, "Goodbye, Nick," just as Sam, the afternoon aide, arrived for his work shift. Kate worked with Nick in the morning, and Sam took over after lunch.

Sam nodded to Kate as she left. Then he walked over to Nick. "Hi, Nick, I'm Sam."

"I'm Sam," Nick repeated.

Nick had never met Sam before, but he found him interesting already. He just happened to be wearing a concert T-shirt promoting one of Nick's favorite bands.

"Okay, Nick, let's get going. What's next?" Sam had worked with Miss Flowers for several years so he was ready to jump right in. However, he would need to get to know Nick better over the next few weeks and establish some trust.

As Nick marked his schedule for sixth period, the bell rang. Nick said, "P.E."

"Yep, that's right. Let's go. Grab your backpack. I'll take you to the locker room." Nick had been attending general P.E. classes since third grade, but the locker room experience was new. Sam helped guide Nick to his backpack, and they headed out the door.

It was a short walk from the 400 Building to the locker room. Entering a locker room full of seventh graders after lunch could be like a trip to the carnival – everybody was excited and high-strung. Fortunately, the new seventh graders were still nervous about their lockers and were busy trying to figure out how to operate their combination locks, so they were relatively subdued.

"Nick, did you bring a lock?" Sam asked as he held up one of the other student's locks.

Lock. Nick looked up at the lock, thought for a moment, and then reached deep into his backpack and pulled out a lock. "Lock."

"Yep, dude. That's right. Lock. Great!"

Before Sam could assist him, Nick had begun twisting the combination dial back and forth. It looked like he was just playing with it, but then, "CLICK," it opened.

"Open," Nick said. Nick and his dad had been practicing operating his lock on and off all summer. He had finally mastered it.

"WOW!" One of the boys noticed Nick's open lock. "Hey, guys, look at that kid! He opened his lock on the first try."

"Did you see how fast he did that? Do it again!" asked another. The rest of the students looked over – their mouths open in utter amazement.

Impressed at the speed with which Nick had opened his lock, Sam exclaimed, "Dude, that's awesome!" Then turning back to the other boys, he said, "Hey guys, I'd like you to meet Nick. He's new here, too."

"HEY, NICK!" they all yelled together.

One boy added, "I remember you from my last school."

In His Shoes

Just then Mr. Glenn, the P.E. teacher, popped his head in the door, "Hey guys, you've got five minutes. Put your uniforms in your lockers and get out to your numbers. No dressing out today."

A collective, "YES!" rose up from the boys.

As the P.E. assistant went around the room telling each student what his roll call number would be, the boys continued getting their locks to work. Once they succeeded, they stuck their P.E. uniforms into the locker and locked it up for the next day. Except for one, most of them were able to open their locks after a few minutes. One by one, they slowly headed out to their roll call numbers.

"Nick Hansen," said the assistant as he looked down his list. "Hmmm, okay, here you are. You're number 23. That means you stand on the painted number 23 during roll call and stretching. See you on the blacktop – number 23."

"DANG IT!" Jarod burst out in frustration still trying to open his lock. "Nick, can you help me? I just don't get it."

Nick just stared blankly down at his hands, flicking his fingers together. Sam sat down next to Nick and explained, "Nick, Jarod needs help. Show him." Then he handed Nick Jarod's lock and a piece of paper showing the combination numbers. "Nick, help Jarod, please. Open his lock."

Nick repeated, "Open his lock." Then he looked at the numbers and back up toward Jarod. Once he fully understood what he was expected to do, he began spinning the dial back and forth according to the numbers on the paper. Soon, "Click," it opened.

"How do you do that? Show me again," Jarod pleaded.

While Sam explained to Jarod how the lock worked, Nick showed Jarod again and again the actual process. Suddenly Jarod got up and said, "YES!

Now I get it. You rock, Nick. Thank you. You are all that and a bag of chips." He put up his hand to high-five Nick but was left hanging solo. Awkwardly, he let his hand fall down to his side and walked away.

Chips? Huh? What the heck? Is he getting me chips? "Chips."

Just then Mr. Glenn resurfaced. "C'mon, guys. Let's go. Line up on your numbers!" Jarod quickly ran out the door.

"Nick, we'll take a short break before we head out to your number," said Sam.

Prior to school starting, Miss Flowers had met with Mr. Glenn to develop a strategy to deal with some of Nick's challenges that might surface during P.E. Understanding Nick's sensory issues, Miss Flowers thought that the locker room might prove to be the biggest sensory hurdle. Thinking back to her own middle school days, she recalled the locker room being a crazy and noisy flurry of activity for a few brief minutes, while the students changed into their uniforms.

"If Nick can arrive a few minutes late for P.E. each day," she suggested, "he would miss that whirlwind of students. It would be much easier for him to get dressed in a quieter environment."

"Perfect. That would work fine," agreed Mr. Glenn. "All he would miss would be roll call. He could still join us for stretching."

"Great. I'll tell his aide our plan, and we'll see how it goes the first week. Thanks," said Miss Flowers.

After that first day of school, whenever it was time for P.E., Nick and Sam would slowly make their way to the locker room, waiting until the other boys had already exited for roll call. Nick would open his locker on his own and get changed. Sam didn't need to help Nick much, except to occasionally remind him of things like, "Nick, don't forget deodorant," which showed as Step #2 on the picture schedule attached to the inside of Nick's locker. Sometimes Sam wished the other boys had a schedule like this on their lockers – the smell of the room led him to believe many of the boys forgot to use deodorant.

Leaving the locker room and walking out onto the black top, Nick was greeted by several kids doing their warm-up stretches. With occasional guidance from Sam, Nick followed the other students stretching.

Soon the noise from the kids began to agitate him, and he started twirling his string on his gym shorts repeatedly. Looking over from number 22, Alli, one of his classmates, noticed and asked Sam, "Why is Nick doing that with his string?"

Sam looked over at Nick then back to Alli and replied, "He does stuff like that when he feels anxious. It's called stimming."

"Stimming?"

"Yes. It's short for self-stimulatory behavior," Sam explained.

"Hmmm. That's kind of weird," Alli commented.

"Well, actually, we all do stuff like this one way or another. Like when you twirl you hair with your finger – like you are doing right now ..." explained Sam.

"Huh?" Alli quickly pulled her fingers out of her hair. "Oh my gosh, I never really thought about it."

"Or look at Mr. Glenn," Sam continued. They both looked towards the teacher. "He cracks his knuckles all the time while he's waiting for you guys to finish stretching. It's just a habit that makes him feel more at ease."

Meanwhile, Nick continued following the stretching routine. At times, Nick was challenged with many of the activities like kicking, jumping or climbing due to what Nick had heard his doctors call his "gross-motor skills." He didn't see anything "gross" about his skills, but he did feel awkward sometimes – kind of out of sync and off-balance. Frequently, his mind would be telling his body to do something, but his body didn't respond appropriately.

Occasionally, he got really frustrated. Then Sam would suggest he take a break. Sometimes Sam adapted whatever activity the students were doing so that Nick could participate with the rest of the class. For example, during baseball, Sam placed the ball on a tee so that Nick would have a better chance of hitting it. Each week, different kids were teamed up with Nick, depending on what they were doing. Most of the kids loved interacting with both Nick and Sam. However, some kids steered clear of Nick, uncertain of his unusual and sometimes "not-so-cool" behavior.

During the third week of school, the students were being individually timed in sprints. Nick stepped up for his turn, and when Sam said, "GO!" he ran as fast as he could – even going quite a bit farther than the finish line. When Nick ran on the track, he felt free and comfortable in his body. It was as if he was a hawk flying, and he didn't want to stop.

As Nick finished his run, Mr. Glenn clicked the stopwatch. His mouth dropped, "HOLY COW! Where have I been? That boy can run!"

Writing down Nick's time, the P.E. assistant noted, "Mr. Glenn, he has the fastest time in this class so far." Looking at the overall stats of the seventh graders, he continued, "Actually, he's in the top five of all your classes combined!"

"I didn't know he ran that fast. Amazing! Hey, Nick, Sam, come here," Mr. Glenn called.

Sam nudged Nick over to Mr. Glenn. "Nick, you are quite a runner. You have one of the top speeds in all my classes combined. You are an amazing runner!"

"Runner," repeated Nick. *Runner*, he'd heard that term before. In fact, he'd been called a "runner" most of his life, but always in the context of a teacher yelling, "He's a runner! Catch him!" or his sister yelling, "Mom, is that Nick running down the street in his pajamas?!" The term "runner" always meant he had swiftly escaped a safe area. Until now, no one had ever used the term "runner" with Nick in a positive way.

"Son, you can run!" Mr. Glenn exclaimed. "Sam, what do you think about Nick being on the intramural track team? Do you think he'd like it?" Without waiting for a reply, Mr. Glenn walked off mumbling to himself. He had already decided to pursue Nick for his track team.

After sixth period, he emailed Nick's mom. "It's a pleasure having Nick in my class. I see some amazing potential in his running ability and would like him to train with our track team. I will provide an assistant. Practice is Tuesday and Thursday for one hour after school. It would be great if you or your husband could attend practice in case we need help understanding some of Nick's needs. What do you think?"

Later that day, Nick's mom emailed back, "Thank you so much. I think it's a terrific idea. I can attend practices with Nick. Please send me all the details."

Mr. Glenn chose Cory, a responsible eighth grader from the other sixth-period P.E. class, to assist Nick during track practice. He knew

he could count on Cory to do a great job. Cory was ecstatic to receive extra credit and was thrilled to have the responsibility of being
Nick's personal trainer.

For one month, Cory was excused from his P.E. class to work with Sam
and Nick during sixth period. Sam gave Cory helpful hints on how to
use visual cards and explained the importance of being direct when
speaking to Nick. He also discussed some of Nick's sensory issues
and showed him how to offer breaks as needed. Also, Sam told Cory
how to anticipate and respond to some of the additional challenges that
would surface at the track meet – like the noise from the starter pistol,
the announcer and the sudden loud cheers coming from the crowd.
Upon Sam's request, Mrs. Hansen provided earplugs for Nick to help
reduce noises he would experience during the competition. As the days
progressed, Cory became more and more involved with Nick while
Sam stood further off to the side observing and offering suggestions as
needed. Cory took the job seriously, but in a fun way.

At track practice the boys conditioned by running together a lot. In addition, they trained for each step in the racing process over and over –
getting on the mark, getting ready, knowing when to start and staying in
the proper lane. Cory had a picture chart and some visual cards attached
to a clipboard that he carried when they weren't running. They took
a lot of rest breaks to make sure Nick didn't get overheated or dehydrated. Nick also wore his earplugs during training to get used to how

they felt while running. Nick's mom provided additional visual aids to help Nick understand every aspect of the race, including the fact that a starter pistol would be shot to signify the start of the race. She also helped out during practice when necessary. She learned more about track in that short period than she had learned her entire life. Nick's parents even took Nick to the sporting goods store to purchase the special track shoes that his teacher recommended.

"What's up, Nick?" they heard as they entered the shoe section of the store. Cory, his "personal trainer," met them at the store to help Nick pick out shoes. "Hey, Nick, check out these track shoes. Just like mine. They're so cool."

"So cool," repeated Nick, looking at the shoes Cory was holding. Then he bounced up and down while rubbing his fingers on the soft texture of the white *swoosh* logo. "So cool."

Once they had found Nick's size, he tried the shoes on and walked around. "What do you think, Nick?" his dad asked. Nick tugged on his arm to lead him out of the store. "I think they're a hit," his dad commented. "Okay, Nick, take them off. We have to pay for them first." But Nick wanted to wear them home and began flapping his hands, agitated that no one seemed to understand him. "No, Nick. You can only wear these shoes during track activities. They're track shoes."

I want to wear them home. Strange noises came from Nick's lips. *Why won't they listen to me?*

"Here, honey, put your shoes in the box. You can carry the box," mom suggested as she helped Nick put his regular shoes back on. They brought the box up to the cashier. When the cashier took the box from Nick to ring up the sale, Nick began flapping his hands again, sensing that he wasn't going to get to keep the shoes.

The cashier quickly scanned the barcode and handed the box back to Nick. He finally understood and felt relieved. "Good luck on your track team," she said with a smile. Nick held tightly on to his new track shoes all the way home. He couldn't wait to wear them the next day during track practice.

As they were leaving the store, Nick's dad turned to Cory and said, "Thank you for everything you've done with Nick. I can tell he likes you a lot."

It was October 29, and Nick's team had its first official track meet of the season. After weeks of training, Nick was finally getting his chance to put all his hard work to the test. They were competing against the other middle schools in the district. Nervous and excited about the competition and the noise of the crowd, he began rocking back and forth, twirling the string on his new track shorts. A classmate who was also getting ready to race noticed what Nick was doing, turned to him and confessed, "I'm a little stressed out too, Nick."

Just before the first race, Mr. Hansen ran up to Nick and made sure he had put in his earplugs. Noticing that Nick was a bit uneasy, he gave him a firm squeeze on the shoulders before heading back to the stands. "Good luck, Nicholas."

Nick smiled and peered sideways, watching his dad walk off into the crowd. Then he looked up and saw Cory at the other end of the track.

Cory stood at the finish line holding a sign that he would flip to a green "GO!" at the same time the starting gun blasted. This way, Nick was also visually reminded of when to start running. "Runners, take your marks!" yelled the announcer. Nick lined up on the starting block like he had practiced so many times before. "Get set!" Nick got his body into the position they had practiced. Suddenly, "BANG!" blasted the starter pistol, and with only a short delay Nick took off running. Although muted, he was distracted a bit by the sound of the crowd screaming and clapping, but did his best to keep focused on running towards Cory. *Run!* He seemed to fly down the lane and quickly caught up to the tail end of the runners, even passing some of them. He came in sixth out of eight kids.

In Nick's second race, the last one of the meet, he felt more at ease with the routine – and more confident. "Runners take your marks!" – "Get set!" – "BANG!" shot the starter pistol. This time there was no delay in his start. Nick shot out of the starting block like a rocket being launched. He blasted passed five of the other runners and came in third!

The crowd from his school went wild. Many of the students had watched him practice with Cory and knew how much effort went into this brief race. Nick covered his ears, but smiled shyly. Peering sideways, he noticed Sarah from his art class on the sidelines cheering. She held a sign that read, "GO, NICK!" He also saw his mom wipe the corner of her eye as his dad raced over to him with open arms ready to embrace him.

Nick leaped into his dad's arms, and soon Karen joined them. "Good job, Nicky," she said, squeezing firmly on his shoulder. Sandwiched between his dad and his sister, Nick held tightly to his ribbon, rubbing his finger across the smooth, satiny material.

"Great job, Nick!" Mr. Glenn yelled across the track, giving him a thumbs-up.

Out of breath, Cory finally caught up with Nick just as he was leaving the field. "Nick, that was incredible. You did it! I am so proud of you, dude!!"

"Dude," replied Nick with a slight smile.

As the Hansen family left the field, Nick looked down at his track shoes and noticed the reddish track dust on them. No longer just a "runner," he was now an official track star.

POINTS TO PONDER ...

 What do you think Adapted Physical Education (A.P.E.) means? Can you think of any examples of activities that can be adapted to help a student with special needs? How might a basketball game be adapted? How about a soccer game?

 How do you think Nick felt when the coach noticed that he was good at running and asked him to be on the track team?

 How could you help a student who might have physical challenges during P.E.? Have you ever assisted anyone in a P.E. class?

 Nick engaged in the "stimming" behavior of twirling a string on his shorts when he felt anxious. Do you ever use these sorts of behaviors to calm you? (What about tapping your fingers, biting your lip or shaking your foot while sitting?) What sort of calming or relaxing behaviors like this can you think of that you may have noticed yourself or others doing?

He's Artistic?

"**B**UZZ!" At the sound of the bell, students dumped the trash from their snacks, grabbed their backpacks and dashed in all directions to their fourth-period classes. It reminded Nick of the gates opening at Disneyland and everyone running in opposite directions to be the first to get to the rides. He just stayed at the table with Kate and watched. When the mad rush ended, Kate got up. "Hey, buddy, toss out your trash. Let's go. Break is over."

Break is over. Nick grabbed his empty milk carton and Twinkie wrapper and tossed them into the trashcan.

"What's next?" Kate asked.

Nick looked at his schedule attached to his binder, ran his finger down the schedule and said, "Art."

Nick's Schedule – Monday

1st Period –
Read a Book/Independent Work
8:00-8:40

2nd Period – Computer Lab
(Ms. Grimm's Lab – Room 205)
8:45-9:25

3rd Period – Speech
(Mrs. Carter's Office – Room 101)
9:30-10:10

Break
10:10-10:30

4th Period – Art
(Miss Smith's Class – Room 401)
10:35-11:15

5th Period – Deskwork & Goals
11:20-12:00

Lunch
12:00-12:35

6th Period – P.E.
(Mr. Glenn's Class – in the gym)
12:40-1:20

7th Period – Sensory/PALs/Games
1:25-2:05

Pack up Backpack and Walk to Bus
2:10

"Yep, Nick, that's right. Let's go see what Miss Smith has planned for today," Kate said as they headed toward room 401.

The walk wasn't very noisy, because the other students had already gotten to their classes. Nick and Kate always got there a bit late for that very reason, but Nick's seat was near the door so it didn't disturb the rest of the class. Sitting in the second row, Nick was also conveniently close to the exit in case he needed to take a break. He loved sitting up near the front, because there were fewer distractions – with one exception: Sitting behind Sarah could sometimes be a bit distracting. He spent a lot of time in class staring at the long curls in her hair while listening to the teacher. Sometimes he had to fight the urge to lean forward and grab one of her curls to see how it would "BOING!" spring back.

Closing her attendance book, Miss Smith said, "Okay, looks like everyone is here today. Good morning, Nicholas. Class, today we have a new student." Pointing at the girl sitting two seats away from Nick, she continued, "Dani just moved here from Virginia. Just like you guys, she likes to hang out at the beach and actually learned to surf last summer."

Raising his hand, Brian interrupted, "Excuse me, Miss Smith?"

"Yes, Brian?"

He's Artistic

"They have a beach in Virginia?" The class couldn't hold back their laughter. Brian looked around embarrassed. "What! What's so funny?"

Miss Smith pursed her lips trying to hold in a smile. "Yes, Brian, they are on the East Coast. Does the Atlantic Ocean ring a bell?"

Nicholas thought, *Does the Atlantic Ocean ring a bell? What a strange question.*

Miss Smith continued, "After class, crack open your geography book and find the U.S. map. Okay, let's move on. Dani has chosen to draw a prickly pear cactus for her project since she has never seen one before. While you are working independently on your art projects, perhaps you can take a quick break and introduce yourself to her."

Nick gazed sideways to catch a glimpse of the new student.

"Okay, so today I want you to pull out your sketches and …," continued Miss Smith.

The sudden high-pitched sound of the leaf blowers outside the room caused Nick to lose concentration and feel agitated. Nobody else in the class seemed to notice. To soothe himself, he began to rock forward and backward and flap his hands. None of the other students reacted, but Nick's movement caught the attention of the new student. Dani turned sideways and stared at him, crinkling her nose in confusion. *Is no one else noticing this guy? What's up with him?* she thought.

"…Time is ticking, so get to work, students," finished Miss Smith.

The kids proceeded to pull out their photos and sketches from their binders. The week prior, Miss Smith had piled stacks of photos all around the room and let them choose a photo to duplicate. Nick had chosen a photo of a hot air balloon taken at a balloon festival. He was drawn to the rainbow-colored balloon set against a clear blue sky. Tami was at Nick's desk showing him her new set of colored pencils. "Would you like to use some, Nick? These colors seem to match the colors of your balloon." Nick looked up and accepted the pencils she held out.

Seeing their interaction, Kate touched a card in Nick's communication book that reminded him to say, "Thank you."

"No problema, mi amigo," said Tami smiling.

Nick loved when she said that. *No problema, mi amigo* reminded him of *The Terminator*. While figuring out which colors to use for his balloon, Nick watched Sarah get up and approach Dani. Her bouncing curls made Nick smile. With colored pencils in his hands, he started to flap and quietly make some noises. Again, only Dani seemed to notice.

"Hey, Dani! I'm Sarah. That's so cool that you surf. I am so jealous."

"Yah, it's pretty fun. I can't wait to try out the waves at San Onofre Beach. I've heard all about 'em," replied Dani.

"Hey, when do you have lunch?" asked Sarah.

"Hmmm, let me check my schedule. Uh, hmmm, oh here it is. I have lunch between fifth and sixth," said Dani.

"Me too! I eat over near the large palm tree if you wanna join me. I highly recommend you stay away from the burgers. They're pretty gross," Sarah added.

Dani looked up and smiled, "That would be cool to have lunch with y'all!" Then she looked over at Nick and whispered rather loudly to

He's Artistic

Sarah, "What's up with that kid? Is he special ed. or something?"

"Oh, Nick? He's autistic," said Sarah, "He's cool. You just gotta get to know him. That's his aide, Kate, next to him. I'll introduce you at lunch, okay?"

Still confused, Dani said, "He's ARTISTIC? I don't get it."

Nick overheard bits of their conversation and was confused also. *Why are they talking about me?*

Sarah giggled quietly. "No, he's not ARTistic – well, actually he is artistic – I said, he's AUTistic. He has autism."

"Autism? What's that?" asked Dani.

"Basically it means he experiences things differently. Loud sounds and lots of activity really bug him, and sometimes he does weird-looking stuff to help him feel better. See that book on his desk?"

"The one with the little pictures?" Dani asked.

"Yah, that's how he talks to us. In pictures. It's kind of like his voice," explained Sarah. "He usually eats near us at lunch so you can ask him about it." Sarah looked up and noticed Miss Smith tapping her watch to suggest she get back to her project. "And – yah. Gotta go. See you later."

"Yah, okay," replied Dani, stealing another glance at Nick, who was working on his drawing. *Hmmm. Autistic. That's a new one,* she thought as she sat back and crossed her legs under her desk.

Nick peered to the side at the new student again, noticing her shoes. *Blue Converse, same shoes as me.* "Same."

POINTS TO PONDER ...

 From what you already know or what you have learned so far in this book, how would you explain or define autism to someone?

 Why do you think it's important for Nick to participate in art class? What other classes that you take might be fun or interesting for someone with autism? How or why?

 If you were in this class, what are some ways you could help Nick? How do you think Nick might be able to help you?

Lunch's on Me

"**B**UZZ!" went the lunch bell as the hands on the clock lined up on the 12. Grabbing the marker on his desk, Nick made a quick checkmark on his schedule. "Lunch!" *Time to eat! Yes!*

To further prompt him, Kate said, "Nick, grab your book. Let's go!"

With his communication book in hand, Nick followed Kate out the door. As they walked through the quad area, he noticed new paintings of turkeys and pilgrims on some of the windows. One turkey, cross-eyed, held a sign that read, "Eat chicken." Nick giggled.

"What's so funny, Nick?"

No response.

"You are a man of many mysteries, Nicholas," Kate continued. "My mystery man."

Nick entered the area near the
lunch tables without appearing to
be bothered by the noise and rush
of activity around him. In the past
couple of months, he had grown
accustomed to many of the campus noises. Even the sudden blasts
from the bell no longer startled

him since he had memorized the schedule and was prepared for each
loud "BUZZ!" That is – except on minimum day schedule. Kate
called it "crazy bell schedule," because on those days the classes
were shortened, and the students were dismissed early. Consequent-
ly, the bells did not follow the usual schedule. Uncertain of what to
expect, those days kept Nick on edge.

As Nick and Kate headed for the lunch area, the lunch line was in
view. Waiting in the lunch line was a challenge for Nick. The way
the kids bunched up waiting to pick up their food was too much
for him to handle. The pushing, jumping, shouting, laughing, teas-
ing and cutting in line overstimulated him, whereas the other kids
seemed to thrive on the blast of energy.

"Nick, over here," Kate called, pointing to a bench off to the side
where they would wait out part of the lunch line each day. Then she
handed him a card marked, "WAIT."

"Wait," Nick responded.

Although he would not have to stand in the whole line, it was important for Nick to learn to wait for at least a portion of the line. Learning to wait was part of his school work.

Kate kept her eyes toward the lunch supervisor. Earlier in the school
year, they had worked out a routine for Nick, and so far it had been

going well. When there were five people at the front of the line, the lunch supervisor signaled Kate to bring Nick over.

"C'mon, Nick. It's our turn to get in line."

Kate gently guided Nick to the lunch line to wait. She held a card marked "**WAIT**" and a strip counting down from 5. Each number on the strip represented one of the five people in line in front of him. Each time a student in front of Nick was served, Kate pulled a number. "Scratch" sounded the Velcro each time a number was removed. Nick could see that his turn was coming soon.

When she removed "1," the bottom of the strip read, "Nick's turn." "Your turn, buddy," said Kate.

Nick's turn. "LUNCH," said Nick.

"That's right. It's time for lunch," replied Kate.

Nick moved forward, grabbed a tray and began to look at the choices. "Chock-Let Milk," he said, picking up a carton of chocolate milk and a salad and putting them on his tray. Then he proceeded to the hot food. After viewing the selections behind the counter, he opened his communication book and pulled out the picture cards representing a burrito and fries. He held up the cards for the lunch lady to see as he had done so many times before.

"Hello, Nick. Burrito and fries comin' right up," she said as she placed the items on his tray.

Kate reached over to Nick's book and touched a card. Nick looked at the card and immediately said, "Thank you" to the lunch lady.

"You are more than welcome, Nick. Have a great lunch."

Great lunch.

Near the cash register, Nick turned to Kate and touched a picture card from his book showing a cookie. Kate smiled and nodded, "Sure, go for it."

He quickly picked up a warm chocolate chip cookie. Smelling the melting chocolate, his mouth began to water. Kate leaned over to his book and pointed at a picture of a wallet. Nick reached for his wallet, opened it and took out his lunch card. Then Kate pointed at the number keypad near the cash register. Nick entered his student number "951306" into the keypad to pay for his lunch. After weeks of practice, he was able to do this on his own with just a little prompting. Lastly, Kate pointed at another card, and Nick said, "Thank you," to the cashier.

"You are welcome, dear," said the cashier.

"Great job, Nick." Kate squeezed his shoulder firmly.

It was finally time to eat lunch!

Lunch's on Me

As they sat down, kids from Miss Smith's art class switched tables and sat down next to them. "Yo, Nicholas, wanna Cheeto?" asked Zach, dangling one in front of him.

"Cheeto." Nick grabbed it and happily chomped away.

Moving closer, Dani asked, "Hey, Kate, can I see Nick's book?"

"Go ahead and ask Nick yourself," Kate suggested.

Dani did, and Nick responded by handing her his book.

"WAY COOL!" Dani said as she looked through the book, which included pictures for the Soak City Waterpark, Pizza Hut and even one for the Nickelodeon Channel.

"Nick, have you ever been to Disneyland?" Dani asked while looking at the book.

Holding his burrito with one hand, Nick reached over with the other to flip the book to a page full of photos of his favorite rides at Disneyland. He tapped twice on the picture of Splash Mountain.

Dani tilted her head. "Huh? Oh, I get it, you like Splash Mountain. Cool! I've never even been to Disneyland. You're so lucky."

"Lucky," Nick repeated.

"He is lucky," Sarah agreed. "Nick's got an annual pass to Disneyland, so he goes a lot."

"He's even been on the new ride," Kate interrupted. "He brought in pictures to show us last month."

"Have you ever been to Disneyland, Sarah?" Dani asked.

"Oh, yah. My family usually takes me every year, but I don't have an annual pass. Maybe next time we go, you can go with us."

"That'd be so cool! I feel like the only person around here who has never been!" Dani responded.

Meanwhile, Kate went over to get some napkins near the cashier. While she was away, a group of kids at the next table started getting rowdy and tossing their ketchup packets across the tables.

"Hey! Y'all, knock it off!" Dani yelled.

Mocking her Southern accent, the boys teased back, "Hey, *Y'ALL* knock it off!"

One boy aimed a ketchup packet at Dani, but it missed her and, instead, hit Nick in the head. Luckily, it didn't really hurt, but Nick became agitated by all the commotion and began flapping his hands and bouncing up and down on the bench.

Another in the group of disruptive students started to laugh, making a crow sound, "Kaw, Kaw, Kaw. Look at Nicholas flapping his hands! He looks like he might take off flying soon! What a moron!"

Moron? No, not a moron, thought Nick.

"Shut up, you idiot. It's not funny! Nick, are you okay?" Zach moved closer to see how Nick was doing.

Still laughing, another kid asked, "What's your problem, Zach Attack? He's not even playing with a full deck. He doesn't understand us anyway."

Full deck? Nick was getting more anxious trying to comprehend why the kid said he wasn't playing with a full deck. Seeing no playing cards anywhere on the table, he tried to sort through this figure of speech. *Full deck?* He could not find the example to match it in his memory bank.

Just then a teacher walked up. "Alright! That's the last straw! Break it up, you guys!"

Last straw? Break it up? Now Nick was really confused. *Where is the last straw? Break what up?* He looked around wondering, *Is this one of those idioms mom always talks about?*

Meanwhile, the teacher sent the rowdy students to the office. Seeing the commotion, Kate hurried back just as the bell rang, "BUZZ!" The rest of the students had dispersed before Kate could find out what had happened.

"Hey, what's going on? What's wrong?"

Kate noticed that Nick was rocking back and forth reciting "Not all treasure is silver and gold, mate," over and over. Something was bothering him. Not knowing what had transpired, Kate did her best to help him relax. The sudden quiet helped, and Nick was able to finish his cookie.

A few minutes later, Nick and Kate began to walk back to the classroom. Kate didn't notice the ketchup packets on the ground and accidentally stepped on one, splashing ketchup all over Nick's shoes.

"Geez, sorry, Nick," she said as she used a napkin to clean up as much as she could. "You are having a bad day, huh?"

In His Shoes

Bad day.

The red ketchup blotches on his shoes reminded Nick of the students who had made fun of him at lunch. He might not have fully understood what they said, but he could tell they were not being kind. *Moron.* Feeling depressed, Nick began making loud noises as he tried to control and understand his emotions.

POINTS TO PONDER ...

 A large majority of kids on the autism spectrum are bullied by others. How can you help prevent this from happening to kids in your school?

 Do you think the kids being bullied understand what's going on, or is it no big deal to them? How do you think they feel? Have you ever been made fun of or bullied and were unable to respond?

 Have you ever witnessed another student being bullied? What did you do? What would you do differently today?

 Why do you think Kate had Nick wait in line instead of getting permission from school staff to skip the line altogether?

 Idioms are figures of speech that, when taken literally, don't make much sense. For example, "the lady has a green thumb" means she's a great gardener, not that her thumb is green. Can you think of some idioms you use that might confuse someone with autism who tends to interpret things literally? How might you reword that idiom so that it would be easier to understand?

Open Wide
and Say,
"Awwwwesome"

Winter break had been fun so far. Karen and Cindy had taken Nick to the Discovery Museum one day, where they spent all afternoon doing activities together. Nick's favorite area was the Pirate's Adventure. He especially enjoyed finding hidden treasures in the digging pit.

Another day, Kate and Sarah surprised Nick by calling to see if he wanted to go to the Disney movie that had just come out. They picked a morning show so that there weren't too many people in the theater. On the way in, they bought a "bottomless" tub of popcorn. This term confused Nick, because they eventually found the bottom when all of the popcorn was eaten.

At times during the movie, Nick went to the lobby for a little while when he felt needed a break, but he was able to enjoy most of the show. Part of the movie was so exciting that he jumped up and down.

On yet another day, Nick's dad took him to the train depot, where they watched the commuter trains coming and going. Each day brought a fun and new experience – until Saturday, then it was …

"Okay, Nicky, let's get going. Time for the dentist!" yelled his mom up the stairs.

Ugh, the dentist. Nick knew it was coming. He'd seen it on the schedule all week, but going to the dentist didn't rank up there with the museum, the movies or the train outing. He tried to forget about it. Going to the dentist rated down there with going to the mall or the grocery store. Just brushing his teeth was unpleasant due to pain and sensitivity in his mouth. The touching and scraping inside of his mouth that a visit to the dentist would involve was literally a sensory nightmare. He let out a long sigh, *Uhhhhh, why today?*

Occasionally, his parents helped him brush his teeth to make sure his teeth and gums stayed healthy. However, lately with the help of a visual sequence chart, he had mastered the skill of brushing his teeth step by step on his own. Today was going to be a big test to see how well Dr. Dave thought he had brushed his own teeth for the past few months.

Nick sat on his bed, not motivated at all for this outing. He pretended not to hear his mom's calls. Soon his mom popped her head in his room, "C'mon, honey. Let's go. We have an eight o'clock appointment. Let's not keep the dentist waiting."

His mom always made the first appointment of the morning so that Nick did not have to sit around the waiting room for too long. Waiting was not a favorite activity for Nick – or his mother for that matter. The concept of time was tricky for Nick to understand. Dr. Dave was really understanding and patient.

Better get this over with, Nick reflected. He slowly put on his shoes and followed his mom down the stairs and out to the car. As they drove down the street, his mom popped in her Air Supply Greatest Hits CD and started singing along. *Ugh, this day is bad enough already,* Nick thought. He tried to tune out the music by concentrating on counting holiday decorations as they drove by. *1, 2, 3, 4, 5, 6, 7...* Time went fast, and soon they rolled into the medical center parking lot where they were able to pull into a front parking spot.

When the car stopped, Nick loudly said, "65."

"65, what, honey?" asked his mom – but she never found out the answer.

Grabbing his iPod, Nick put on his headphones. Turning on his music helped him relax and block out the annoying noises he anticipated at the dentist office. He also remembered to put his sunglasses into his pocket. Nevertheless, he could feel his anxiety creeping up on him as they walked through the office building entrance.

As they entered the empty lobby, Nick took a deep breath. The receptionist looked up with a smile. "Good morning, Mrs. Hansen. Hello, Nick. Good to see you. We'll be with you in just a moment."

Just a moment, thought Nick. *What is a moment?*

In His Shoes

"Okay, Nick we need to sit down and wait for a while," explained his mom, handing him a small card marked, "Wait."

While waiting, Nick listened to his iPod. His mind flashed back through some of his past experiences at the dentist's. He remembered when he was young; prior to the visits, his mom would show him a story in pictures that explained step-by-step how the appointment would progress. It had helped to know ahead of time what to expect.

His thoughts mixed the good with the horrible visits. Just a few years ago, a trip to the dentist office was like riding a terrifying roller coaster. His fear of the unknown, the noise of the loud drills and the actual pain involved were nerve-racking for him. Sometimes he reacted by lashing out at people. On one visit, while the dentist worked in his mouth, the pain became so intense that Nick bit the dentist to get relief. He had no other way to communicate his pain.

He had come a long way since then. He didn't necessarily love going to the dentist, but now he knew what to expect and did his best to remain calm. He had grown up a lot. It also helped to have people there who supported him. The visits were no longer roller coaster rides – more like bumper cars with Nick in the driver's seat of his own car.

Snapping out of his flashback, Nick saw the door to the inner office open. Becca, the hygienist, smiled, "Hello, Nick. C'mon back. We're ready for you."

Ready for you. Pretty smile. Nick's mom nudged him out of his chair, and he followed Becca.

Walking through the doorway, his eyes squinted in reaction to the painful glare from the office lighting. Fortunately, he had brought his sunglasses. *Ahhhh, much better,* he thought as he put them on.

Open Wide and Say "Awwwwesome"

After he was seated in the dental chair, Becca placed a special heavy-weighted x-ray blanket on him. He wasn't having x-rays taken during this visit, but the blanket applied even pressure to his body, which made him feel more comfortable. The dentist had learned this "trick" when Nick was younger.

"How's that, Nick?" asked Becca.

"How's that Nick," he echoed.

"Is it okay?"

"Okay," Nick answered, his eyes glancing in the direction of the dental water gun.

Becca's eyes followed Nick's to the water squirter, and she was reminded that squirting the water was one of Nick's favorite activities. They even had targets in the bowl for the kids to shoot at. She opened up Nick's medical file and pulled out a "First/Then" card. The card showed a small photo of a child getting his teeth cleaned over the word **"FIRST."** She added a small photo of the water squirt gun over the word **"THEN."**

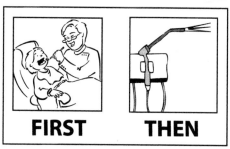

FIRST   THEN

Smiling, she pointed to the card and said, "Okay, buddy, *first* we clean your teeth and *then* you get to squirt the water gun. Deal?"

"Deal," Nick said with a grin, his hands starting to flap a little.

While Becca cleaned Nick's teeth, she checked off boxes on a "countdown chart" that showed him how they were proceeding

91

through the appointment. Each time she checked off a number that brought them closer to the final number, zero, Nick knew that it was almost his turn at shooting the water squirter.

"Almost there, Nick. Just one more to go."

When she checked off the last number, Becca touched the "All Done" card.

Following her every move, Nick smiled with relief, "All done!"

Finally, Becca handed the squirter to Nick, who giggled as he shot water at the targets in the bowl. Becca set a small timer for three minutes. When the timer rang, she said, "Okay, Nick, all done. Let's have Dr. Dave check your teeth."

When the appointment was over, Nick's mom joined them to discuss Nick's progress.

Dr. Dave announced, "Nick, you've done a super job cleaning your teeth, buddy. You have no cavities! That's terrific."

"Terrific," said Nick as he stared mesmerized at Dr. Dave's Peanuts character tie.

Dr. Dave showed Nick and his mom a picture chart that detailed a few areas where Nick's mom could help Nick do an even more thorough job of keeping his teeth clean.

Dr. Dave said, "Nicholas, I'm going to give you these special flossing sticks to help you start flossing regularly." To Nick's mom he added, "You may need to create some sort of chart to help him with this."

"No problem. I'm the queen of picture charts," Mrs. Hansen replied.

The dentist then handed the package of flossing sticks to Nick.

Interesting, thought Nick as he observed the flossing sticks in his hands. He opened the bag and pulled two out. They were shaped like little swords and reminded him of *The Pirates of the Caribbean,* his favorite Disney movie. He put one in each hand and pretended to sword fight as he imagined tiny pirates fighting each other. *You may kill me, but you may never insult me! Who am I? – I'm Captain Jack Sparrow!*

At the end of the appointment, Dr. Dave gave Nick a high-five and said, "Great job, Nick! Go pick out something from the teen treasure box."

Nick wandered over to the box and picked out a McDonald's gift card. He hoped his mom would take him to get a Big Mac meal for lunch, so he pulled out his communication book and showed her a picture of a hamburger with fries and said, "Fries, please."

"You got it, Nick," Mrs. Hansen responded smiling, adding to the receptionist, "Well, I guess we are headed to the golden arches this afternoon!"

Nick was proud that Dr. Dave thought he did a great job on his teeth brushing. Plus, he was thrilled to be headed to McDonald's. He had a little bit of a skip in his step as he walked out of the dental office. "Fries, fries, fries …"

POINTS TO PONDER ...

🐾 Do you enjoy going to the dentist? If not, what bothers you?

🐾 Do you remember the dentist's office EVER being scary or overwhelming? How did you make yourself more comfortable during the appointment or how have you overcome some of those fears?

🐾 Why do you think it is important for Nick's parents to teach Nick to take care of his own teeth?

🐾 The dental office had a lot of areas that could cause sensory issues (sight, sound, smell, touch, taste). Take a moment to look around the room you are in. Do you notice anything that might bother someone with autism with regard to sensory issues?

🐾 Why do you think the concept of time and waiting might be difficult for someone with autism to understand? Sometimes people's comments regarding time can be unclear or imprecise. Try to think of the following statements and discuss how they might be confusing to someone with autism:

"Wait a second. I'll be right back."

"Just a moment."

"Come on, hurry. Let's get on the bus. Okay, now wait."

"You can finish the puzzle later. It's time for math."

"It's time for lunch. Go wait in line."

"I'll be there in a minute."

A Prism of
Promise

*S*unday, *YES,* thought Nick as they arrived in the church parking lot. He loved going to church. The only thing he didn't like was that his mom always wanted him to "dress nicer," which meant he couldn't wear his soft P.E. uniform with a pair of perfectly worn-in Converse. She preferred that Nick wear his "Sunday clothes," which included wearing his stiff khaki pants and his brown leather shoes.

"Karen, honey, can you take Nick to junior church while we set up the coffee for fellowship time?" asked Mrs. Hansen.

"No problem. I'll meet you in church. C'mon, Nicky," Karen willingly agreed.

In His Shoes

As they got out of the car, Karen stayed with Nick, helping him navigate the parking lot. She had to grab his arm firmly to pull him out of the path of a passing car. The driver smiled and waved at them as she drove past. Entering the walkway, Nick ran his hands across the stained-glass windows lining both sides, admiring the vibrant colors and mix of textures.

In the garden, he scrambled away from Karen to touch the smooth marble statues and watch the bubbling fountains. *Water.* He placed his hand under the stream of water and watched it flow through his fingers as if counting each molecule. *Amazing.* He could spend hours in this restful home-away-from-home. The calmness of the garden gave Nick a sense of peace and acceptance.

After giving Nick his "garden time," as Karen called it, she guided him toward the church buildings crossing paths with Frank, the youth pastor. Leaving Nick with Frank, Karen headed over to talk to a friend.

"Hey, Nick-O! Where's my high-five?" Frank held up his hand waiting for Nick to respond.

Nick returned the high-five. Then he lifted his hand and twisted his index finger on his cheek showing the sign for "candy."

"Oh, so, you think I have candy, huh? Well, use your words, Nick."

Candy, Nick thought spying the bright-red package sticking out of Frank's pocket. Trying again to get the words passed his lips, he thought, *Candy.*

"C'mon, Nick. You can do it. I know you can. Use your words. I want …" Frank pulled out the candy from his pocket showing him the package.

A Prism of Promise

"Candy, please!" Nick finally blurted out. *YES! I did it!*

"Good job, buddy. Here you go. Skittles, your favorite. All for you. See you later."

"Later." *Mmmmmm,* he thought ripping open the package and admiring the rainbow of shiny candy in his hand.

Karen looked up just as Frank handed Nick the Skittles, "I gotta go. See ya," she said, turning away from her friend and calling out to Nick. "Hey, it's time for junior church. Let's go." Then, as she started guiding Nick towards his classroom, she waved, "Catch you later, Frank."

As soon as he had entered the classroom, Nick found a puzzle and brought it over to a table where he quickly sat down and started on the puzzle right way. As Karen signed Nick into class, Amy, the class helper, walked up to them. "Morning, Nicholas. Hey, Karen, what's up?"

"Not much, Amy, how 'bout you? Doin' anything for spring break?"

"Nope, just hanging out with Rachel. We'll probably hit the beach a couple of days. We'll have to take the bus though 'cause my parents are working. Wanna go to the mall with us one day?"

Rachel, Amy's older sister, was 22 and had Down Syndrome. Amy usually watched out for her, but Rachel pretty much took care of herself. She was one of the teachers in the Sunday preschool class down the hall and had a job at the local library.

"Sounds like a great idea," Karen said. "Forget the bus. I think my mom can take us. She took the week off. Call me later." Hearing the church bells, Karen headed off to the church services.

In His Shoes

Nick was busy with his puzzle while the rest of the kids settled in. The class included fifth through seventh graders. None of the kids attended his school, because the church was located quite a ways from Nick's home. The Hansens used to attend a church just down the street from their house, but when Nick was three and his autistic behaviors surfaced, the church board had told Mrs. Hansen, "Your son's behaviors are not manageable, and we aren't equipped to care for him." The family no longer felt welcome, so they sought out a friendlier environment for Nick and had found a wonderful new church where they felt accepted as a family.

When it was time for class to start, Amy came over to Nick with a card marked "WAIT." She gently placed the card on top of the puzzle and said, "Time for the lesson, Nick. You can finish the puzzle afterward."

Nick was a bit frustrated, but he trusted Amy to let him return to the puzzle later. She handed him a stretchy Koosh ball to hold to help him relax during the lesson and also had a "BREAK" card available for Nick on the table.

While the teacher was talking about the rainbow representing God's promise to Noah, Nick felt like he needed a break, so he picked up the "BREAK" card and handed it to Amy. He said, "Break" and they got up and left the room. After a brief walk through the garden, they returned to the class. By this time, the kids were busy gluing together a rainbow craft.

"Hey, Nick, over here. I started yours for you," said Kimmie, one of the other students in the class.

A Prism of Promise

Nick sat down next to her, and they worked side-by-side gluing the foam pieces together, creating rainbows to hang from the ceiling. Nick didn't like the sticky feeling of glue on his fingers and kept trying to wipe it off. When he was finished with his craft, he turned to Amy and said, "Puzzle."

"Great job, Nick. That's right! You can finish your puzzle now."

Kimmie looked over and noticed Nick working on his puzzle at an incredible speed, "Wow, Nick. You are amazing!" She worked on her own puzzle, but not quite so fast.

When Nick finished, Kimmie asked, "Nick, can you help me do my puzzle?"

Puzzle. "Puzzle."

"Nick, Kimmie wants help with her puzzle. Scoot over; you can work together," Amy suggested.

He did, and they finished just as the church bell gonged, "BONG, BONG, BONG …" signaling the end of the worship service. Nick heard the church bell and thought, *All done.*

"Thanks, Nick," said Kimmie. "I don't know how you can do these puzzles so quickly."

Amy made a trumpet call with her mouth announcing, "And now, class, introducing Mr. Nicholas Hansen, master puzzle maker of room 303." The other kids clapped enthusiastically.

Just then Nick's dad came by and signed him out. Nick practically galloped out of the room, headed for the church patio for refreshments. He had barely made it to the snack table when he saw the familiar lavender hair. Smiling, he thought, *Roxy.* He always remembered her name, because her grey hair had a tint of lavender, which reminded him of the purple *rocks* in his fish tank at home.

As the elderly lady approached Nick, she began talking to him really **LOUDLY** and very s-l-o-w-l-y, "Well, hello, Nicholas Hansen. How are you today?"

Why do people talk to me like that? I'm not deaf! I just need more time to think. "How are you today?" Nick repeated.

"Oh, I'm fine, honey. I saved you something. Here's a yummy rainbow-sprinkled donut just for you."

My favorite. His mouth watering, Nick stared. "Donut."

"That's right, donut. Here you go, sweety."

"Sweety," he repeated.

"Well, aren't you adorable," Roxy responded.

After spending a brief time on the patio, Nick and his family got ready to leave. Nick returned a wave goodbye to Frank. As they walked out to the parking lot, Nick noticed a strange squeaky sound coming from his feet. He covered his ears to block out the annoying sound. He had forgotten he had on his leather shoes, which made a funny noise when he walked. As soon as he got into the car, he flicked off his shoes. *Ahhhhhh, that's better.* He couldn't wait to get home and put on his flip flops.

POINTS TO PONDER ...

 Why do you think some people speak loudly and slowly when dealing with people with disabilities?

 If you were out in the community (at the park, the mall, a sporting event, a church function, etc.), what are some ways you could make a person who might need assistance feel more welcome or comfortable?

 During junior church, Amy provided some assistance to Nick. Can you think of ways you could help someone like Nick in your classroom or during community activities?

Dancing the
Day Away

"Beeeeep, beeeeep, beeeeep, beeeeep" echoed the bus Monday afternoon as it backed up, letting Mrs. Hansen know that Nick was home. As she opened the door and waved at the driver, Nick trotted off the bus wearing his headphones and carrying his backpack. Barely acknowledging his mom with a millisecond of eye contact, he walked right past her and into the house, where he promptly tossed his backpack in the middle of the entryway. Then he turned on the TV and headed for the snack his mom had ready for him.

"Teenagers," Mrs. Hansen muttered as she picked up her son's discarded backpack. Then she proceeded to open it to check for notes from Nick's teacher.

A yellow flyer stuck out. She read the bold headline, "Seventh-Grade Spring Dance, Friday, April 24, at 2:30 p.m." About to toss the note, her eyes were immediately drawn to a handwritten note from Kate that read, "Mrs. Hansen, I'd like to chaperone Nick to the dance. Several of the kids he knows will be there. I think he'll enjoy it. If it's okay with you, you can pick him up at 4:30 that afternoon right in front of the multipurpose room. Let me know what you think."

Great idea, thought Nick's mom and sent a note back to Kate.

"Looks like you are going to your first dance, slugger," she announced to Nick. But Nick was in his "TV world" and didn't appear to hear.

First dance, slugger. He'd heard alright!

The following day, Kate received Mrs. Hansen's enthusiastic response and let Miss Flowers know that she would be taking Nick to the spring dance. Miss Flowers was thrilled. "That is terrific, Kate. What a great opportunity for Nick. What do you think about priming Nick prior to the dance?"

"What is *priming*?" Kate asked.

Miss Flowers explained, "*Priming* is kind of like viewing the preview for a new movie. You see little clips and then know what to expect when you see the real thing. You show Nick picture-by-picture activities that will take place at the dance. It gives him a heads-up, and he'll be less anxious about the overall experience."

"That makes sense! Will you help me?" asked Kate.

Dancing the Day Away

While the students were busy looking at books, Miss Flowers showed Kate how to use a computer program to create small picture cards. Kate flipped through various pictures on the computer before selecting some that were relevant to the upcoming dance. Later, she laminated each card to make it sturdy and attached the cards to a thick plastic strip with Velcro. This way Nick could simply pull a card to show Kate what he wanted to do at the dance. Also, she printed a special "break" card that Nick could show if he needed to take a break. Kate made the strip narrow so it would fit in Nick's pants pocket for easy access.

"Perfect, Kate," Miss Flowers said when Kate showed her what she had come up with. "I'll make a smaller version of each picture card, too. I'll laminate them and attach them on one of those stretchy keychains," she suggested. "I'll ask Sam to review them with Nick every day prior to the dance."

"Great idea," said Kate. "Oh, and aren't the PALs here on Monday and Wednesday afternoons? They might enjoy reviewing the cards with Nick."

"Perfect!" replied Miss Flowers.

Each day prior to the dance, Sam showed Nick the pictures and talked about the upcoming dance. In addition, the PALs had a blast reviewing the schedule with him and asking him to pull off the cards for various activities. They kept showing him the "Friends" card and pointed at themselves. Nick smiled and looked down at his strip.

107

In His Shoes

When Nick came into the classroom the morning of the dance, he immediately noticed something had changed on his regular Friday schedule. The area that usually read "Pack up Backpack" was scratched through and now read "Take a Break." In addition, a 2:30 time was added. It read, "Spring Dance with Kate." There was a picture card showing kids dancing.

At first he rocked with anxiety at seeing the change to his schedule, but as Kate walked up to show him the dance picture strip again, he remembered why there was a change in his schedule.

"Today's the big day, Nick. Your first dance," announced Kate.

"First dance," he echoed.

"Nick, is that a new outfit? Looking good, buddy. I'm going to have to hold back the girls today," teased Kate.

"Girls today."

"Yep, that's right, girls today," confirmed Kate anticipating a fun afternoon with Nick. She realized there might be some difficulties, but she felt Nick could handle the new activity and was thrilled for him.

Later when the 2:10 bell rang, Nick checked off his schedule and saw Kate entering the room to take over after Sam's shift ended. Nick smiled. Kate usually attended college classes in the afternoon, but she had no classes on Fridays. She was excited to see how Nick would like this new experience and hoped that he felt ready for the dance.

"Have a blast, buddy," said Sam as he left. "See you Monday."

"See you Monday," Nick echoed.

"Later, Sam," Kate said, turning to Nick. "Okay, Nick, let's take a quick break and head over to the multipurpose room. Remember, it's the big dance today."

On the way to the multipurpose room, Kate found a quiet area where Nick could relax before they entered the dance. The potential for sensory overload was high, and Kate's goal was to prevent it. They reviewed the picture strip one last time, and she gave him the keychain with the duplicate picture cards. After hooking the keychain to his belt loop, Nick flipped the cards around with his fingers, briefly looking at each one.

"Remember, Nick. You get as many breaks as you want. Your break card is easy to find. Look, it's yellow," Kate explained, showing him the card. "Are you ready?"

Am I ready? Am I ready? "Ready," Nick answered.

As they entered the multipurpose room, Nick handed a teacher his ticket. At first he and Kate stood off to the side so he could take it all in at his own pace. *Good music*, he thought. He was mesmerized by the colorful lights darting all over the walls from the disco ball in the center of the room. *Awesome!* With a smile on his face, he began to jump up and down. Kate watched him carefully and could tell Nick was just excited, not anxious – yet.

As they started to walk farther into the room, Sarah approached. "Hey, Nick, wanna dance with us? Come on!"

Nick recognized her. *Sarah. Pretty hair*, he thought. When he was with Sarah, he got a tingly feeling in his body that he had never felt before. He wasn't sure what that was all about, but it wasn't bad. It made him feel good. Flipping through his keychain cards, Nick found the one marked "dance" and showed it to Kate.

In His Shoes

"I think he'd love to dance with you guys.
I'll be right over here if you need me,"
Kate said, pointing to a chaperone table a
few feet from the dance floor.

"Great, let's go, Nick!" shouted Sarah above the
music. She put her hand out and Nick grabbed it
as she led him to the dance floor.

Nick seemed to be having a great time. He fit right
in with the other kids dancing. Kate wished she had
brought a camera. Later she noticed that someone from
the yearbook class was taking pictures, so she made sure
to suggest that they include Nick in some of the photos.

All the kids had their own dance moves, and Nick's
were really good. It was great seeing him enjoy himself with his classmates. It didn't hurt either that they
were playing some of his favorite music. Nick even
joined in when the DJ played the *Macarena* song. She thought, *Ob-
viously, he's done that before!*

Soon more and more kids entered the dance floor, and the music got
louder and louder. When the DJ made announcements, the volume
became too much for Nick. He covered his ears, closed his eyes and
stopped dancing. Noticing his reaction, Kate got up and headed over to
him. She reached for his keychain and touched the yellow "break" card.

"Break," said Nick, and the two of them quickly grabbed a soda and
went outside for a break.

Throughout the afternoon, Nick came and went from the dance as he
enjoyed the food, the dancing, the kids and the music. A break here
and there enabled him to stay for most of the event, but by 4:15 he
was ready to go home. He pulled the "All Done" card, and he and
Kate went out in front of the school to wait for his mom.

110

Dancing the Day Away

As Sarah was leaving, she looked up and noticed them sitting on a bench. "Hey, Nicholas, you won a prize! They called your name during the raffle. I saved it for you. Here ya go."

Kate gestured for Nick to say, "Thank you."

"Thank you," he quickly responded.

"You're welcome, Nick. Did ya have fun? I did. See ya Monday. Bye, Kate."

As Sarah left to catch up with a bunch of friends, Nick removed the wrapping paper from his prize to find a new CD. He immediately recognized the picture of the artist and tapped his finger on the case. He couldn't wait to listen to it on the way home.

Handing the CD to Kate, he said, "Open."

"Open it, please," Kate reminded him.

"Open, please."

Kate opened it up and handed it to Nick for the ride home.

When Mrs. Hansen pulled up, she thanked Kate for taking Nick to the dance. Then she cautiously asked, "How'd it go?"

Kate smiled. "Great! I think he had a super time. He even won a prize! See you Monday, Nicholas."

"BaBye," responded Nick.

On the way home, as Nick listened to his new CD, Mrs. Hansen noticed his sneakers tapping to the beat of the music he had heard at the dance. *Awesome!*

POINTS TO PONDER ...

- How do you think a picture strip or keychain like the one Kate reviewed with Nick prior to the dance might help him?

- What are some areas at your school or in a community environment that might cause sensory overload (too much noise, strong smells or flashy visuals)?

- What could you do to make a student with autism (or any other disability) feel more welcome at a school or community activity? If you feel nervous approaching the student, what would make you feel more comfortable?

- Do you think that people with autism face some of the same issues you face? What are some examples? Do you ever get frustrated when places you visit are too noisy? Have you ever been involved in something (like a school activity or a project at home) that stressed you out so much that you needed to take a break for a moment?

Clean-Up on Aisle One

As Nick walked with Sam out the school gates to the bus stop, Mrs. Hansen drove up and lightly tooted her horn to get their attention. Rolling down the window, she said, "Hi, guys! Hey, Sam. How have you been? I got off work early today and thought I'd pick up Nick on the way home."

"Hello, Mrs. Hansen. Doing great, thanks. Is your family doing anything special for Memorial Day weekend?"

Nick quickly got into his mom's car. "Home."

"No, nothing special. How about you? Any exciting weekend plans?"

"Home," repeated Nick. No one responded.

In His Shoes

"I might go to the river with some friends, but I haven't decided yet. You guys have a good weekend. I gotta run before all this carpool traffic blocks me in," Sam added as he waved goodbye.

"Okay, bye!" replied Mrs. Hansen and headed out of the parking lot towards home.

Two streets down the road, Nick noticed that his mom had missed the turn that would take them home and again said, "Home." As she made yet another turn that was definitely NOT taking them toward home, he repeated, "HOME" – only this time louder.

Finally, tuning into Nick's comments, his mom said, "You're right Nick. I missed the turn to go home. We have to go to the grocery store to buy a few things for dinner. It'll only take a minute."

"Minute. Home," Nick repeated. He felt a drop of anxiety hit his belly.

"Yes, honey. It will just take a minute," his mother reassured him, trying to remember the few items she needed to get.

"Minute," Nick whispered, looking at the digital clock on the dash-board. *2:33.*

As they pulled into the grocery store parking lot, Nick looked at the clock again. *2:43.* He let out a heavy sigh. "Minute."

Luckily, they got a close parking spot so they didn't have to walk far. As they approached the store, Nick watched the automatic glass door glide sideways. *Interesting!* After Mrs. Hansen had found a grocery basket, she suddenly noticed that Nick was no longer with her. He was still watching the door glide back and forth as customers entered and exited steering around him. *Wow!*

As his mom came back out to redirect him into the store, Nick watched the door open again. *How does that work?* Knowing that her son could stand there forever watching the automatic doors, she finally grabbed his hand and guided him into the store with her so quickly that he barely had time to look up and view himself on the security monitor at the front of the store, as he always did. *Hey, slow down, mom.*

Once inside the store, all Nick's senses immediately went on high alert. *Ouch,* he thought as the flickering lights sent stabbing shots of pain into his eyes. Instinctively, he reached into his pocket for his sunglasses. *Where are they?* he wondered. Taken aback by this un-scheduled stop on the way home, he had left them in the car.

"So, Nick, let's make this quick; do you want chicken or spaghetti tonight?" Mrs. Hansen urged.

No response.

Too bright. Too loud. Can't hear mom. Shopping carts rattled, music blared, customers chatted on cell phones … *Shut up!* He covered his ears and rocked back and forth as his mom selected a favorite brand of spaghetti sauce.

"Okay honey, hang on. Just one more thing. Uhh-hhh – French bread. That's it. Then we're all done."

"All done," Nick echoed as they passed the seafood counter. *Okay, let's go home now, mom.* "Home."

The smell of seafood made his stomach swirl with nausea. He thought he was going to be sick, but his mom rushed him to the bakery. Here she quickly grabbed a bag of fresh bread, and they headed toward the cash registers.

By this time, all the sights, sounds and smells were getting to be too much for Nick. He felt like a balloon being filled up with each new sensory experience. There was no relief to release the pressure. "Puff, puff, puff" – more sensory stuff entered until there was no more room in his "sensory pressure" balloon. It was going to pop if he didn't get relief very soon.

As Nick practically ran toward the front of the store followed by his mom in hot pursuit, other customers turned to see what all the commotion was about. When they finally reached the check-out lane, Nick was rocking wildly. Customers stared at his unusual behavior.

"Momma, what's wrong with that boy?" asked a wide-eyed little girl.

"Shhh, it's not polite to stare," replied her mom as she dragged her to the next check-out lane.

Nick's anxiety continued to increase. "Puff." Suddenly Nick noticed a DVD he wanted, and his sensory pressure seemed to decrease a tiny bit. "Sssssssssss." He picked up the DVD and put it into his mom's basket, but she immediately put it back on the rack. Feeling misunderstood, Nick grabbed it again. "Puff, puff, puff," into his balloon. His emotions, frustrations and senses began exploding as he blurted out the word, "MOVIE!"

"Oh, God. Nick, not now, please," Mrs. Hansen pleaded under her breath. "We just need to pay for these items and then we'll go home and eat dinner."

Clean-Up on Aisle One

At the sound of those words, one more puff of air entered that imaginary sensory balloon, "NOOOOOOO!"

"POP!" The balloon was finally stretched too thin and burst. Nick's sensory cork had officially popped.

"No! No! No! No! Noooooooo!" he screamed and cried, flopping himself onto the floor right in the check-out aisle. He began kicking his legs aggressively.

Mrs. Hansen thought, *Oh no, not a meltdown now! Not here. C'mon, Nicky. Hang in there. We're almost done.*

An elderly lady behind them muttered, "What a spoiled brat."

Behind her, a young mom holding a baby loudly whispered back, "You wouldn't catch me putting up with that."

As Nick continued to kick his feet, he accidentally knocked a bunch of items off of the sales rack, including a small bottle of pink, gooey candy, which spilled all over his shoes. Mrs. Hansen got down on the floor with Nick to ensure he didn't hurt himself or anyone else around them.

A young man approached from the other side and offered, "Is there anything I can do to help?"

"No, but thanks for offering," Mrs. Hansen said in an exhausted voice. She was about to cry but told herself, *Hold it together. He needs you!*

Hearing the commotion, Marco, the store manager, came over. He recognized the situation – and Mrs. Hansen – and looking down at her, he mouthed silently, "It's okay." Then turning to the customers behind her, he said with a smile, "I'll help you all over here on aisle three."

Somewhat relieved Mrs. Hansen turned to her son. Without speaking, she did her best to gently manage his flailing legs while waiting for Nick's "sensory balloon" to deflate. Talking was useless. It could even make things worse. After a few minutes, the kicking stopped. She waited until Nick's breathing was under control before speaking.

Finally, she asked, "Are you okay, Nick?"

Okay. "Okay."

While Nick was still recovering on the floor, Mrs. Hansen reached up and handed the cashier a wad of money. Exhausted, she apologized, "I'm so sorry. Please charge me for this candy, too. Do you have a towel?"

Still unsure of what she had just witnessed, the young cashier finally closed her gaping mouth and said, "Uhhhh. Oh, uhh, it's no problem, ma'am. Don't worry about it. We'll get that cleaned up later. Here's your change. Uh, thanks." She handed Mrs. Hansen the shopping bag.

Bag in hand, Mrs. Hansen helped her son up and ushered him out of the store past the gawking customers, whose eyes followed them all the way to the door. As they left, she saw Marco look up with a sympathetic smile. She silently mouthed, "Sorry," back to him as she rushed Nick out the sliding glass doors.

As soon as they had gotten into the car, Nick's eyes immediately shifted to the dash board. *3:10. Not a minute, mom. Not a minute.*

On the way home, Nick thought back upon the trip to the grocery store. He was completely exhausted. He heard sniffles coming from his mom and looked over to see tears flowing down her cheeks. He reached his hand over and gently touched a tear. Then he stared at his moist finger.

Clean-Up on Aisle One

When they pulled up in their driveway, Mrs. Hansen wiped her face with a tissue, thinking to herself, *Pull it together!* With puffy eyes, she turned to Nick and, letting out a sigh, said, "Nicky, I know you wanted that DVD. We'll figure out a way you can work for it this week." Slowly reaching out and clutching his hands, she put her forehead to his forehead, "Nick, I'm sorry that we didn't go straight home today. I also screwed up by not bringing your communication book into the store with us. Baby, you know I love you, right? I love you, Nick."

I love you too, Mom. "I love you, Nick," he repeated.

Her eyes drifted down, "I'll help you get that sticky candy off your shoes, okay?"

"Okay," he repeated. At the mention of his shoes, Nick looked at the pink stains with sad eyes and thought, *I feel bad. Mom is sad. I hate when that happens.* "Shoes."

POINTS TO PONDER ...

 What sort of visual (things you see) or auditory (things you hear) things are there in a grocery store that might bother someone with autism? Do any of these things ever bother you in a store?

 What other community places might pose similar "sensory" challenges for someone with autism?

 How do you think Nick's mom felt during his "meltdown" in the store? How do you think Nick felt just before his behavior got out of control? How do you think the other customers or the store employees could have helped in this situation?

Best Gift of All

"**G**ood morning, sunshine! Guess what day this is?" Mrs. Hansen practically bubbled with excitement as she danced into Nick's room. Barely awake, Nick squinted as she opened the blinds and let in a steady stream of light. As if that wasn't enough, she then flipped on the CD player, and soon he heard the Beatles blasting, "They say it's your birthday ..."

Nick rubbed his eyes, cracked a big yawn and smiled. He recognized the Hansen birthday tradition in action. It was June 13 – his fourteenth birthday!

Today's the day! "PARTY! PARTY! PARTY!" Nick repeated in a monotone voice.

As she sat down on Nick's bed, Mrs. Hansen thought back over the past few weeks of planning.

In His Shoes

Nick's birthday coincided with the end of the school year, which meant that summer vacation was always the best gift of all. Each year the family did something fun to celebrate. Nick's ninth birthday, at Pizza Party Palace, was a disaster, because they had overlooked his sensory challenges. There were too many children running around, the fun zone was bubbling over with loud noises, and it smelled like a grease pit. For Nick, it was more like Supreme Sensory Station. Every year they learned a little more about how to help him celebrate in a way that he would appreciate. One year, when Nick was interested in trains, they celebrated his special day by taking him on a short train ride to his favorite restaurant, the Spaghetti Factory. His mom even called ahead and reserved a dinner table in the trolley car.

As Nick headed to the bathroom to take a shower, his mom got up to make his bed. She thought back to a family meeting they had a few weeks prior. They were all browsing through pamphlets and websites brainstorming for birthday ideas. Suddenly Nick pulled out one and seemed to be studying it intensely.

Karen noticed. "Nick, you like that one? Let me see it." She moved next to him to look at the brochure he was holding. "Wow, that's cool! Hey, mom, dad, listen to this one." She read the brochure out loud, "It's the Reptile Wranglers. 'We'll come to your house and throw a wickedly awesome reptile party.' Nick seems to like it. What do you guys think?"

"Ahhh, that looks really neat. I think Nick would like that," Mr. Hansen replied.

His wife interrupted, "Snakes and lizards! What about the kids who would be grossed out?" She paused, "Or the moms, for that matter!" *Snakes, ugh!*

Nick chimed in, "Snakes and lizards."

"Hon, I think you are outvoted," Mr. Hansen laughingly turned toward his wife. "Tell you what. We could have them set up on the side yard, out of the way. I'll even have them count the critters when they arrive and make sure they leave with the same number! No stragglers."

"All right. I surrender. I'll call them and see if they are available on June 13th," Mrs. Hansen said heading for the phone.

Meanwhile, her husband continued, "The trampoline will be a fun activity for the kids. Right, Nick? What do you think about the trampoline?"

Nick was listening intently. "JUMP!" he said

"Okay, that's a *go* then," his dad announced.

"Karen, can you have some of your friends come help that day?" He bribed, "I'll take you all out to Starbucks after the party? What do you say?"

Mmmmmm, Vanilla Bean Frappuccino Blended Cream. Yum. "I'll check with the kids at church to see if they are interested. If it all works out, we can wear our red youth shirts. That way the kids will know we are helpers and not party crashers. What do you think, Nick?"

Engrossed in the Reptile Wranglers brochure, Nick didn't reply.

"I'll take that as a *yes*," said Karen.

Just then Mrs. Hansen put down the phone and returned with thumbs-up. "It's all set. June 13th it is, Nicky."

Filling her mom in about the plans they were working on, Karen asked, "Mom, what do you think about me setting up a sensory table for the kids? You know – bowls of dried beans, rice, slime, that kind of thing? The kids can sift through the stuff with their hands."

"Sounds great. Remember Nicky's third-grade Open House when his teacher had that sensory bin full of stuff to taste? I wonder if the kids would like that, too?" her mom asked.

"Ooooh, Mom, cool idea! I can buy those Mega Warheads Sour Sprays and, hmmm, Hot Tamales Fire, Pop Rocks, and, oh yah, Squeeze Pops, Sour Skittles …"

Her mom interrupted, "Karen, that sounds great, but don't go overboard. We want the kids to have fun, not go flying high on sugar."

"Okay, it's set then," Mr. Hansen chimed in. "Right?"

"RIGHT!" they all echoed.

"Yah, uh, except – who should we invite?" Mrs. Hansen asked.

There was a tiniest moment of silence in the room – and perhaps a bit of a groan. Inviting was tricky, because not only would Nick need assistance doing the inviting, knowing whom to invite was sometimes a mystery waiting to be solved. Nick didn't have friends IMing him on the computer. He didn't make or receive phone calls from classmates. He didn't have buddies texting him on a cell phone. Socializing was very challenging for him.

Just then, Karen's eyes lit up and she said, "Hey, I have an idea!" She grabbed Nick's communication book and brought it over to the table. Flipping through it, in the section marked "PEOPLE," they saw pictures of family, school staff, classmates and PALs. "Nicky, who do you want at your party?" asked Karen, pushing the open book towards her brother.

But Nick didn't seem interested. Indifferent, he headed to the computer and logged on to the Internet.

"Well, I guess it's up to us to figure it out," Mrs. Hansen said.

She finally decided to send a stack of invitations to school with a note for Nick's aides asking them to help him distribute the invitations to students on campus whom they felt were close to Nick. She suggested the PAL students and also the track team, specifically Cory. She also decided to email some invitations to the parents of some of his church friends.

"Okay, all set. Now, cross your fingers," she said as she finished up.

"All set," Nick quietly repeated as he searched for music on iTunes.

Hearing the shower shut off, Mrs. Hansen's mind popped back to the present "Nick's 14," she mumbled under her breath. "Hard to believe how time flies."

Then she left his room and went downstairs to finish preparing for the party.

Just before noon, Mrs. Hansen took one last look around to make sure everything was ready. The house did not have the typical look of a party. There were no balloons, because just the simple *possibility* of one of them popping was enough to cause anxiety with Nick and his classmates. There were no loud party favors and very few decorations. From the patio, she could see Karen and her friends putting the finishing touches on the sensory table. They were testing out the Sour Skittles. *Neat kids. We're so lucky.* Mrs. Hansen walked around the trampoline just to make sure everything was safe. Then she headed to the side yard where the Reptile Wranglers were already in action. Nick was getting a private preview of all the creepy, crawly critters, *UGH! Snakes. Mental note, stay clear from that area today, gross.*

In His Shoes

Heading back to the kitchen, she looked over the refreshment table and saw everything was ready to go. *Pizza is on its way.* She took one last peek into the quiet room they had set up in the den. *Beanbag chairs, yoga ball, soft mats, calm music. This will be a nice break area for Nick's classmates.*

"Okay, it's show time!" she whispered to herself, crossing her fingers.

"Ding dong," the doorbell rang as the first guests arrived.

Nick was bouncing on the trampoline, while his mom greeted each guest. As his classmates arrived, she told their parents that they were welcome to stay and that otherwise their child would be assisted by one of Karen's friends during the party. "Is your child on a special

diet? ... Let me show you the quiet room we set up over here ... See the kids in the red t-shirts, they are my daughter's friends ..." Nick's mom had everything carefully planned.

"Hey, Nick," yelled Karen. "Turn on the CD player. Let's have some music."

Nick practically leaped off the trampoline and bounced into the house. He pushed a few buttons on the CD player, and soon the music was playing. As some of the PALs arrived, they split up to try different activities.

"Hey, Nick!" yelled Zachary, entering with Mr. Hansen through the side gate. He took the stack of pizza boxes Mr. Hansen was juggling and headed for the food table to drop them off.

After locking the gate, Nick's dad turned and yelled, "PIZZA, KIDS!" Trying to beat the kids to the food, Mrs. Hansen ran into the kitchen and pulled a pizza out of the oven – an extra one she had made for the kids who were on a special diet. Soon most of the guests were happily munching away.

"You sure pulled off a nice party," Riley's mom complimented. Peering over at the stack of gifts, she pointed and added, "How are you going to handle that challenge?"

"We already talked about this to prevent any problems," Mrs. Hansen replied. "We told Nick that we would open the gifts at the family party afterwards. We put it on his schedule for tonight at seven o'clock. It's just too much for him, and everyone else for that matter, to deal with this afternoon. I hope that doesn't sound rude," she concluded.

"Not at all. It sounds smart," Riley's mom replied.

In His Shoes

"Later on Karen's going to work with Nick to create thank-you notes on the computer. My sister sent him a new graphics program for his birthday so he'll be excited to try it out."

"Very smart. I gotta hand it to you. This party is definitely a success. Last year for Riley's 13th birthday party, we went to Pizza Party Palace and …"

"You don't have to say another word. Been there, done that! Disaster Central. We call that place Supreme Sensory Station," laughed Mrs. Hansen.

Riley's mom added with a laugh, "That's definitely a more fitting name. Oh, looks like Riley is getting a bit agitated. Do you mind if I take him to the quiet room?"

"Of course, not. That's what it's there for."

Every now and then, Mrs. Hansen noticed Nick going off to his bedroom for a few minutes to take a break, but then he'd bounce right back and join the party. He even appeared to enjoy just watching others have a good time. He paced around the backyard watching Cory and Miguel jumping on the trampoline while also observing kids digging their hands into the slime on the sensory table.

"C'mon, Nick, join us," called Karen. Nick came over right as Karen sprayed some Sour Spray candy on Eva's tongue. Eva's face went all squinty and then she laughed out loud and said, "MORE! MORE!"

"More, more," Nick said, so Karen sprayed his tongue, too. He left the area all squinty faced and giggling.

Rounding the corner, Nick saw Sarah and Zach with the Reptile Wranglers. Zach was taking a picture of Sarah holding a snake.

"Nick, get in the picture with Sarah." Zach helped Nick move a little closer to Sarah and then snapped a photo.

"Wanna hold the snake?" asked Sarah.

Just as he was going to respond, he was distracted.

"HEY KIDS! It's cake time. Come over here. Let's sing 'Happy Birthday' to Nick," said Mrs. Hansen.

"Cake time," said Nick.

Nick ran over and quickly counted the candles, *2, 4, 6, 8, 10, 12, 14!!* He smiled as the cake was set down before him. It was covered with reptile figures and rock candy. *Awesome.*

The kids all joined together to sing "Happy Birthday," and Riley helped Nick blow out the candles. Nick pulled a candy rock off of the cake and tossed it into his mouth. *Yum.*

"Here, Miguel, want these?" Karen asked as she removed the reptile figures from the top of the cake. Miguel grabbed them, licked off the frosting and began lining them up in a straight row.

Eva sat next to Miguel, happily munching on a special gluten-free, casein-free cupcake.

As the party began to wind down, Nick thought back through the day and whispered quietly, "Happy Birthday." It was terrific to be with family, friends and yummy food. Then as he looked over at his classmates and some of the PALs jumping on the trampoline, he burst out, "JUMP!" took off his sneakers, threw them into a pile and ran to join them. "JUMP!"

POINTS TO PONDER ...

- What were some of the differences you noticed in this party compared to traditional birthday parties you have attended? How might those differences help someone with autism?

- Do you think you might have had a good time at Nick's party? What activities would you have tried?

- Why did Nick's parents have him wait until the guests were gone to open presents?

- At a traditional birthday party, what are some things that might cause someone with autism to become anxious or overwhelmed?

- Do you think having some "typical peers" (like the PAL students) attend the party was important to Nick?

The Rainbow Connection

urray! Finally, it was the last day of school! Miss Flowers' class had a small party in the afternoon and invited the PAL students to join them. Several of the students flocked around Nick.

"Nick! Your party was so cool," said Sarah. "I'm still dizzy from the trampoline! I gave Sam a note for you to take home to your mom. Do you think you could meet some of us next Wednesday at Cold Stone Creamery?"

"Ice cream," replied Nick. His stomach rumbled at the thought of Oreo cookies smashed into vanilla ice cream. *Mmmmmmmmm.*

"Yep, we'll meet for ice cream," Sarah confirmed.

After visiting with the other students, Zach came up to Nick, "I brought you something, buddy. It's a little scrapbook with pictures from this year, including your party. I hope you like it. Will you be at the community center this summer? I'll miss you, bud."

"Miss you, bud," echoed Nick.

Opening the book, Nick thought, *This is great.* Each photo had a caption with it. Looking at the photos, he thought, *Computer class. Track team. Lunch tables. Shoes.* Nick couldn't wait to take this home to show Karen. She could help him read some of the words he didn't recognize. He looked at one of the photos showing Zach with his arm around him. It simply stated, "Friends."

"Friends," Nick said quietly recognizing the word.

As the PAL students were starting to leave the classroom, Sarah came by and told Nick, "Have a great summer." She slowly reached out her hand. Nick reached out and held her hand.

Curls. "Great summer," he echoed back.

The group of PAL kids were gathering just outside the doorway, and Nicholas could hear part of what they were saying as he thumbed through his scrapbook.

Mr. Michaels, the PAL coordinator, asked, "Did you all enjoy your year in the PAL program?"

A resounding, "YES!" followed.

"Mr. Michaels?"

"Yes, Sarah?"

The Rainbow Connection

"I thought that we were going to be teaching these kids a bunch of stuff this year. I feel like we let them down. It's like I learned more from them," Sarah said confused.

"Sarah, there's an old saying, 'If you walk a mile in someone's shoes' ..."

Sarah interrupted. "I know; I know. My mom always says that, 'If you walk a mile in someone's shoes,' you'll understand them better."

Nick stared out into the hallway at Sarah. *Why would someone want to walk a mile in another person's shoes? What's wrong with their shoes?*

"Mr. Michaels, I agree with Sarah, did we teach them anything?" Tami asked.

"The PAL program is not just about you guys teaching other kids stuff. It's about building relationships and understanding ..." Mr. Michaels continued as the group left the building.

Nick tried to direct his listening away from the hallway and back to the classroom where Miss Flowers had put some relaxing music on the CD player. Meanwhile, he flipped to the last page of the scrapbook and beamed. Zach had taken a picture of the colorful rainbow of shoes that were stacked up in a mountain next to the trampoline during his birthday party. The kids had all taken off their shoes to jump. There was a fantastic collection, including colorful Converse, bright flip flops, sparkly heels, black sandals and red-checkered Vans. Each pair of shoes was unique, and yet together they were like a work of art. He treasured this photo – and his first year at middle school. The caption read ...

POINTS TO PONDER ...

 The teacher used the idiom "If you walk a mile in someone's shoes," which confused Nick. Do you know what that figure of speech means? How could you translate that saying into something that would be easier for Nick to understand?

 Looking back at Nick's first year in middle school, what were some of his challenges? What about his successes?

 What is the most important fact or lesson you learned on this short journey through Nick's first year at middle school?

 What did that stack of shoes represent to you? What do you think the caption for that last picture should read?

Glossary of Terms

ADAPTED P.E. (A.P.E.): A form of physical education that is modified to address the individual needs of children and youth who have delays in gross-motor development. For example, in a game of basketball, the hoop might be lowered to assist a student in successfully shooting a basket.

AMPLIFIED: When sound is turned up loud. Kids with autism sometimes can't adjust the volume or tune out sounds in their ears so what sounds "normal" to you might be extremely loud in their ears.

AUTISM: A neurological disorder that affects how the brain works and causes people to experience the world differently from the way most others do. People with autism can have a hard time communicating with others and expressing/understanding emotions. In addition, they may find social situations challenging. They might also exhibit repetitive behavior. Autism affects a wide variety of people each with his/her own unique abilities, gifts and challenges.

AUTISM SPECTRUM: Describes the range of autism disorders from severe, classical autism, to Asperger Syndrome, often called a milder form of autism. An individual diagnosed with severe autism exhibits many noticeable behaviors and symptoms such as hand flapping, rocking and lack of eye contact in addition to sensory issues and more extreme communication and social challenges. A person with Asperger Syndrome has no delay in verbal language or intellect, but might find social and emotional interaction tricky and could experience sensory challenges. The thinking and learning abilities of people on the spectrum can range from severely challenged to gifted.

CDC: Centers for Disease Control and Prevention – a U.S. government agency that is part of the Department of Health and Human Services. Among other things, they report research statistics for autism and other disorders or diseases.

COMMUNICATION BOOK: Book used by someone who is challenged by expressing himself using words. It might contain pictures (and/or a combination of written words) of various things, places, food items and emotions. Someone who is nonverbal could show the pictures to let others know what he is thinking, feeling or wanting. The book enables the person to express himself or communicate needs without necessarily being able to talk.

ECHOLALIA: When somebody repeats back words or phrases spoken to him instead of responding or answering. For example, if a teacher asks a child, "How are you today?" and the child responds with the same question instead of saying, "I'm fine."

GESTURE: The act of moving part of your body (for example, pointing your finger toward something) to help express thought or to emphasize speech. Pointing your finger at a chair where you want a student to sit down is a gesture, as opposed to telling her in words to sit in the chair.

GLUTEN-FREE, CASEIN-FREE: A special diet that some people with autism follow to help them feel better and improve their responses, behavior and perceptions. This diet eliminates gluten (specific proteins found in wheat and other grains) and casein (proteins found in milk).

GROSS-MOTOR SKILLS: These include the ability to control the large muscles of the body for walking, running, sitting, crawling and other activities. The muscles required to perform gross-motor skills are generally located in the arms, legs, back, abdomen and torso.

IDIOMS: Figures of speech that mean something in a certain culture, but when taken literally (word for word) don't make much sense. For example, "Don't let the cat out of the bag" means don't tell the secret. It has nothing to do with a cat being set loose from a bag.

IEP: Stands for individualized educational program. An IEP describes the educational program created specifically to meet a child's unique needs. In the United States, by law, each child who receives special education and related services must have his or her own specially designed IEP. A special IEP team (teachers, parents, administrators, related services personnel and students as appropriate) comes together to work out a program that benefits the student and helps him or her do well in school.

INTEGRATING: In Nick's situation, integrating means going from his special day class into other classes with "typical" children. For example, he was "integrated" into art, P.E. and computer classes and worked with the students enrolled in those classes.

NONVERBAL: Basically refers to someone who communicates without using words. A student who is nonverbal might use picture cards, sign language or a keyboard to communicate. Sometimes individuals considered nonverbal repeat back words/phrases (echolalia) and have some limited speech, but are unable to effectively communicate through verbal language (words).

PERIPHERAL VISION: Utilizing the visual perception that occurs at the edges of the field of view. When Nick peers off to the side instead of turning his head and focusing his eyes directly, he is using his peripheral vision.

PRESSURE: Uniformly applying force to an area. For some individuals with autism, a slow, steady application of pressure on certain parts of their bodies has a calming effect. For example, some kids with autism like to be rolled up in mats or blankets for pressure. Some like to have steady pressure applied to their head.

PRIMING: A strategy that makes it possible for students to preview information, events or schedule changes prior to a situation actually occurring. Students are shown materials ahead of time to prepare them for an upcoming activity as a way to reduce the stress level they might experience when the actual activity takes place. It's especially helpful for those who require structure and predictability. For example, if a special assembly will be added to the school schedule, a teacher might present this information to the student several times on the days leading up to the schedule change.

PROMPT: A cue or hint meant to induce a person to perform a certain behavior. A prompt can be made in words ("go get your book") or with a gesture (pointing at the book) or even by hand-over-hand (holding the child's hand while you both pick up the book). For instance, when Kate wanted Nick to pay for his lunch, she *prompted* him by showing him a picture of a wallet.

Glossary of Terms

SELF-STIMULATORY BEHAVIOR (STIM): Repetitive body movements or repetitive movements of objects. For example, when Nick was nervous, he would twirl the string on his gym shorts. Rocking back and forth and flapping are also examples of "stimming."

SENSES: The five senses include sight, sound, smell, touch and taste. The information we received from our senses helps us understand and navigate our world. When discussing senses, some people also include vestibular (sense of balance) and proprioception (relating to the position and movement of the body). Individuals on the autism spectrum can experience sensitivity to sounds, lights, fabrics and can be resistant to the textures in some foods. Some are overly sensitive (over-reactive), and some are insensitive (under-reactive) to certain senses.

SENSITIVE: Easily or strongly affected or even hurt. For example, some kids with autism feel a lot of pain or uneasiness when brushing their teeth because their mouth is *sensitive* to touch.

SENSORY ISSUES: When a person has challenges related to the senses (sight, hearing, taste, touch and smell). For example, too many visual distractions in a room (such as flickering lights, vivid posters and a fan rotating) can make a child with autism feel overwhelmed. Also, certain smells, or combinations of smells, can cause a child to become nauseated. Sensory issues might also include feeling "underwhelmed" or not reacting to something. For example, the child might not react to the noise of a pot crashing down onto the kitchen floor or feel much pain when he has hurt himself.

SENSORY OVERLOAD: When one or more of the five senses are experienced to an excess and it becomes difficult to focus on the task at hand. While Nick was at the grocery store, he was experiencing sensory overload with all the noises, visuals and smells "attacking" him all at once.

SEVERE AUTISM: Type of autism with very noticeable symptoms and behaviors (such as lack of eye contact, spinning, rocking or lining up toys). People with severe autism often have challenges learning to talk as well as learning social skills like playing with others. Some people with severe autism experience mental challenges and are unable to communicate effectively using spoken words. Instead they may use keyboards, sign language, visual picture cards or written words. They may experience many sensory issues.

SOCIALIZING: Interacting with other people.

SUPPORTS: Items that help make learning easier and assists with behavior challenges. For example, a card with a student's schedule listed in pictures and/or words on his desk would help *support* him in knowing what comes next on the schedule in class.

VERBALIZE: Ability to speak or express ideas and feelings using words.

VISUAL SUPPORTS: Picture-oriented tools that help support kids with autism. Visuals come in many forms, including pictures, physical objects or words *shown to* students to help support their learning. For example, a picture card of a lunch bag could be used to show a student it's time for lunch. Also, a written countdown of numbers (5,4,3,2,1) could show a student he has five more math problems, then four more problems left to do, and so on, so that he can see an end to the assignment. We all use visuals, such as calendars, to-do lists, etc.

VISUAL THINKER: A person who tends to think in pictures in his mind rather than in words. For example, Nick's class desk schedule shows pictures along with the words. Sometimes the pictures are helpful if the words are confusing or unknown. Also, Nick's communication book includes picture cards, which enable him to use pictures (or visuals) to communicate with his family, classmates and school staff. Many people with autism are visual thinkers.

Would You Like to Learn More?

For more information about autism and autism awareness, take a look at the following pages.

The Internet, your local library and neighborhood bookstores are terrific places to find out more about autism. If they don't have the materials you seek, maybe they can order them for you.

Websites

The following websites are great resources for kids and teens regarding autism and autism awareness.

A Is for Autism, F Is for Friend
This author's webpage contains activities and links for kids to learn more about autism.
www.AisForAutism.net

Autism Society of America
ASA is a national organization that provides information on autism and is a leader in supporting autism research. The site also provides links for those in the autism community.
www.autism-society.org

Daniel Hawthorne's Webpage
Posted on this site is a variety of childhood memories written by an individual who experienced life growing up on the autism spectrum.
tbns.net/danielrh/cotf.html

Fitting In & Speaking Out: Me and Asperger's Syndrome
A young man with Asperger Syndrome speaks out describing the advantages and disadvantages he faced as an individual with autism.
www.hoagiesgifted.org/fitting_in.htm

Growing up Together ASA Bridges 4 Kids
A printable booklet that explains autism and provides helpful hints on how to become friends with a child who has autism.
www.bridges4kids.org/pdf/Growing_Up_Booklet.pdf

Would You Like to Learn More?

Kid's Health – Information for Kids on Autism
This kid's health site details what autism is and how it is treated.
www.kidshealth.org/kid/   (search autism)

Teen Health: Autism
Teen health site which includes brief tips and topics regarding autism.
www.kidshealth.org/teen/   (search autism)

Thinking in Pictures – Temple Grandin
An in-depth essay written by an individual with autism detailing her
life as a visual thinker.
www.grandin.com/inc/visual.thinking.html

Wrong Planet
A web community and online resource designed specifically for individuals on the autism spectrum which includes articles, discussion
forums and chat rooms.
www.wrongplanet.net

Recommended Books

Clark, J. (2005). *Jackson Whole Wyoming*. Shawnee Mission, KS: Autism Asperger Publishing Company. Upper-elementary school novel follows the ups and downs of a fifth grader, Jackson, who has Asperger Syndrome and his budding relationship with a classmate. (ISBN 1931282722)

Clark, J. (2007). *Ann Drew Jackson*. Shawnee Mission, KS: Autism Asperger Publishing Company. A sequel to *Jackson Whole Wyoming*, this story follows the unexpected blossoming of a friendship between a boy with Asperger Syndrome and a strong-willed young girl. (ISBN 9781931282451)

Elder, J. (2005). *Different like me: My book of autism heroes*. London: Jessica Kingsley Publishers. Introduces children to famous, inspirational individuals with autism from the world of science, art, math, literature, philosophy and comedy. (ISBN: 1843108151)

Gagnon, E., & Myles, B. S. (1999). *This is Asperger Syndrome*. Shawnee Mission, KS: Autism Asperger Publishing Company. Through vignettes and illustrations, this book introduces siblings and peers to the challenges faced by children with Asperger Syndrome. (ISBN: 0967251419)

Heiman, H. (2007). *Running on dreams*. Shawnee Mission, KS: Autism Asperger Publishing Company. Written from the perspective of two middle school boys – one with autism and one typical – the novel presents how their relationship builds from turbulent to friendship. (ISBN: 1931282285)

Would You Like to Learn More?

Keating-Velasco, J. (2007). *A is for autism, F is for friend: A kid's book on making friends with a child who has autism.* Shawnee Mission, KS: Autism Asperger Publishing Company. Presented from the perspective of a young girl with autism, this book provides a discussion-oriented introduction to autism for typical peers. (ISBN: 9781931282437)

Larson, E. M. (2008). *The chameleon kid. How to control meltdown before he controls you.* Shawnee Mission, KS: Autism Asperger Publishing Company. Using a cartoon-like format, this illustrated book addresses issues related to preventing and controlling behavior meltdowns. (ISBN: 9781934575222)

Levine, C. (2007). *Jay grows an alien.* Shawnee Mission, KS: Autism Asperger Publishing Company. In this short novel, a young boy with Asperger Syndrome faces challenges, but also finds that his differences are unique and special. (ISBN: 1931282293)

Notbohm, E. (2005). *Ten things every child with autism wishes you knew.* Arlington, TX: Future Horizons. A mother of a child with autism presents a quick read which highlights the perspective of the child with autism by covering ten key areas. (ISBN: 1932565302)

Recommended DVD

Hoy, R. (Director). (2007). *Autism and me* [DVD]. London, England: Jessica Kingsley Publishers. Award-winning short film by Rory Hoy, an 18-year-old who has autism. Provides a brief video journey into his world of autism. (ISBN: 1843105462)

APC

P.O. Box 23173
Shawnee Mission, Kansas 66283-0173
www.asperger.net